D0553240

DEAR JOHNNIES . . .

DEAR JOHNNIES . . .

THE 2 JOHNNIES SOLVE ALL YOUR PROBLEMS

Johnny B and Johnny Smacks

Gill Books

Gill Books
Hume Avenue
Park West
Dublin 12
www.gillbooks.ie

Gill Books is an imprint of M.H. Gill & Co.

Text © Johnny B and Johnny Smacks 2019
978 07171 8791 1

Design and print origination by O'K Graphic Design, Dublin
Illustrations by Kate Gaughran
Copy-edited by Djinn von Noorden
Proofread by Susan McKeever
Printed by ScandBook, UAB, Lithuania

This book is typeset in 12/17 pt Minion
With chapter headings in CCsezYou

The 2 Johnnies are the hugely popular comedians Johnny B (O'Brien) and Johnny Smacks (McMahon). From Tipperary, they were brought together by a love of music, comedy and GAA. They are the hosts of the phenomenally popular *2 Johnnies Podcast*. Together they have had five number-one singles, as well as a sold-out live tour.

CONTENTS

Introduction

The GAA

Boundaries

Going to College

Partying in College

Jobs

Moving to Dublin

Moving Abroad

Holidays

Fashion

Having a Baby

Social Media

Acknowledgements

CONTENTS

Introduction   1

The GAA   7

Housemates   27

Going to College   45

Dating in College   65

Jobs   81

Moving to Dublin   97

Moving Abroad   117

Holidays   139

The Gym   155

Having a Baby   175

Social Media   193

Acknowledgements   209

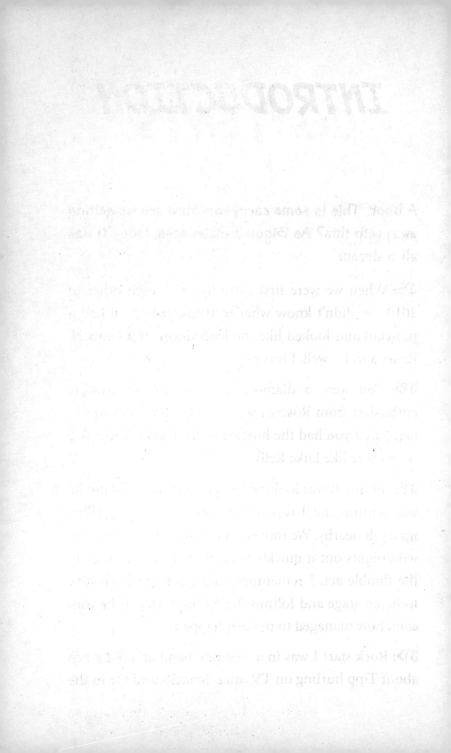

INTRODUCTION

A book. This is some carry-on. How are we getting away with this? As Biggie Smalls says, lads, 'It was all a dream.'

JS: When we were first introduced to each other in 2010, we didn't know what to think. Johnny B had a ponytail and looked like the lead singer of a Guns N' Roses and I – well, I was …

JB: You were a diamond-earring-wearing Westlife enthusiast from Roscrea who told anyone who would listen that you had the hurling skills of Eoin Kelly. You were more like Luke Kelly.

JS: Johnny B was looking for a lodger in the house he was renting and I was new to the area, having taken up a job nearby. We moved in together and after a few wild nights out it quickly became clear we made quite the double act. I remember telling Johnny B I'd love to be on stage and Johnny, being the rock star he was, somehow managed to make it happen.

JB: Rock star? I was in a wedding band and did a rap about Tipp hurling on TV once. Smacks told me in the jacks of the Hill Inn one night that he would be on the cover of *Heat* magazine someday. Some people want to be an astronaut, Smacks wanted to be a D-list celeb.

We can honestly say that when we first set foot on stage together at the local pantomime in Cahir back in 2015 (where we wrote our own parts for a five-minute parody that made no sense in the context of the show because we didn't read the script) we had no idea that we'd be sat here together writing a book.

From the panto came the bright lights of Cahir House Hotel in early 2016, where we hosted our club's local Strictly Come Dancing and went full Ant and Dec – the dance moves, the 'Let's get ready to rumble' soundtrack and the matching suits. That was the lightbulb moment for us and so 'The 2 Johnnies' were born. Not much imagination went into the names. And to answer the most common question we get asked: 'Yes, both of our names are actually Johnny.'

An auld fella and his wife approached us after that gig and said, 'I'd say you're onto something there with that craic.'

We decided to set up an online page and we published our first video to Facebook on 31 May 2016 (which shows us commentating on a titanic battle between our club, Cahir, and the mountain men from Golden in the under-21(B) football county final). Everyone at the game thought we were crazy, and they were right. We'd just like to take this opportunity to apologise to the Golden number 10 who we referred to several times by saying, 'There's a fair bit of rearing gone into him.' Anyway, the video went viral and so did we.

This was the start of us building an online presence on Facebook, YouTube and the rest through the videos, sketches and of course the songs that somehow, at the time of printing, have managed to get us six Irish number ones. Each week on our day off we'd film a sketch in the hope of maybe one day making this our full-time job and maybe a long career. It wasn't too far away.

JS: I remember one Monday, which was my day off from being your local friendly butcher in Dolan's SuperValu in Cahir. (I'll expect a free steak for that!) I called up to Johnny B's to film a sketch, as was the routine on a Monday. We'd just started to earn a few pound from doing shows in GAA clubs and the like. I told him I was thinking of quitting my job and that we could give this a right good go. If we failed, sure what about it? I was a qualified butcher and could always go back at that. The next day I arrived up to the house to tell him I'd quit my job and I was broke so he better get his finger out.

JB: He arrived into my kitchen, with the big John Travolta walk on him, and tells me, 'I've quit the job.' Hands out in the Jesus Christ pose, like he's just kicked the winning penalty for Ireland in the World Cup. I said, 'Ah lad, bit soon for that.' We were filming sketch comedy on our phones, a selfie stick taped onto a mic stand. Genius. Not exactly Hollywood. But if Johnny Smacks is anything, it's ambitious. And confident, he's super confident, absolutely sure we're going to make it, not sure about the hard work needed to get there! A fella on Facebook wrote, 'Your parachute won't open unless you jump.' I don't know anything about parachutes, but anyway, we made the jump.

It turned out to be a good choice. Since then we've performed in sold-out venues like Dublin's Vicar Street – yes, we did end up in Coppers – as well as doing shows all over the world, from Abu Dhabi to Ballylanders via San Francisco.

Another big moment that changed the game for us was on 19 February 2018, when the first episode of *The 2 Johnnies Podcast* was unleashed. We wanted to talk about the things you wouldn't hear on radio, represent the real people of Ireland, the man in the van, the man in the tractor, the man in the truck, the man on the bike (shouldn't be listening to headphones on a bike, ya hipster), the woman hunting kids out to school, the

4

students, the commuters, the girls getting ready for a night out, the many Irish abroad who listen to keep in touch – that first episode went in at number one and it's been there pretty much ever since.

So back to the book. If you're a fan of the podcast and having a bit of craic, then this is the book for you. If not, then it's too late, unless you're one of the people who goes into Eason's and reads the first few pages to see if they like it. If you're one of those people, then please buy this book. It's actually decent.

'Dear Johnnies' is a segment we do sporadically on *The 2 Johnnies Podcast*, to help out damsels in distress or, as we like to call them, people from Carlow. People say we give good advice, although our mothers were traumatised to see us dishing out sex advice on The Late Late Show Valentine's special. Mammies, we're sorry. And that's what this book is. It's giving the ordinary people some advice on a range of problems including relationships, social media and moving to Dublin. So sit back, relax and enjoy the book – and genuinely thanks so much for supporting us this far. Now go on and sort your life out.

Disclaimer: Please remember the advice given in this book is by two guys: one hangs teabags on the washing line he's so tight and the other wears shorts in winter.

Basically, if you take the advice and it doesn't work, don't come crying to us. SPILT MILK.

THE GAA

Dear Johnnies,

I need yer help with this one and I know that Smacks has gone through this as well, so it's probably right up yer street. I'm from Co. Cork and am a real GAA man. I played all my life with my hometown club from under-6s to senior. Last month I made the big decision to move to Kilkenny for two reasons: 1) The love of a good Kilkenny woman. I know ye're from Tipp but don't hold that against me and 2) I got a job promotion in work, which meant I had to move to our head office, which is based in Kilkenny.

While this was great news for me personally and the girlfriend, it was bad news for my hometown club. I love the hurling and still want to play, and I feel I have a lot to offer. I tried to continue playing for my hometown club in Cork but the commute was killing me. Last month I took the plunge and transferred to a club here in Kilkenny. We start back training next month and I'm wondering could ye guys give me some tips on how to fit in at my new club and how can I impress my new club mates? Appreciate yer help, lads. Hon the rebels!

Thanks a million,

Mickey Doyle

Co. Cork

Mickey, ye're a brave man. Leaving the hometown club is never easy. Some will call you a Judas but don't mind your immediate family – they'll get over it someday. Bedding into a new club can be tough but that's where we come in, and by implementing the following advice you can't go wrong:

Don't oversell yourself

JS: It's important not to oversell yourself when it comes to your ability. No one likes a Champagne Charlie. I've learned this the hard way. When I first transferred, I spent all pre-season telling the squad I was the next Eoin Kelly. I turned out more like Luke Kelly. I mean, I could hold a tune and could play an instrument but unfortunately that instrument wasn't a hurley. I probably shouldn't have told them I was a fantastic free taker. It's easy to say it, doing it is another thing. Trust me, don't open your mouth because when you're standing over a free to win the game and you can feel the eyes of a whole parish staring at you – it's shit or bust. I stood over the ball thinking I could be the hero or I could be about to receive dog's abuse. I received the latter.

You should grow a thick skin fast, Mickey, because getting abuse from the locals in the stand is part and parcel of being a local GAA player. These are the kind of insults you should prepare yourself for:

You're nothing only a blow-in

Meaning: a blow-in is a person who's moved to a new town. You'll be seen as a blow-in for at least the first five years in the parish, so get used to hearing this.

You couldn't hurl spuds to ducks / You couldn't beat eggs with a whisk

Meaning: your hurling ability isn't to a high enough standard and you're incapable of hitting a spud into a pond.

You wouldn't finish your dinner / You wouldn't find eggs in a hen house

Meaning: you lack the ability to finish the ball to the net or over the bar.

Jesus he wouldn't go into a dark room that fella / He's watery / Jesus that fella is yella

Meaning: you're afraid to challenge your marker and are not physically tough enough for the game.

You wouldn't catch a cold

Meaning: you lack the skills to catch the ball.

IMPRESS AT YOUR FIRST TRAINING SESSION IN YOUR NEW CLUB

JB: Your reputation at your GAA club is like your virginity. Once it's gone, it ain't coming back.

You only get one chance to make a first impression.

The gear you turn up in can say a lot about you. There was once a hurler in our club who trained in all white. Full Roger Federer job. White socks, shorts, T-shirt and helmet. You could see it in the eyes of the farmers. They didn't know exactly why they hated him, but one way or another they were gonna kill him. You won't have any of the club gear, so wear a jersey or training top from your home county. Everyone likes jerseys and it'll start a few conversations.

A guy I knew turned up to hurling training wearing a helmet that had two black ridges down the middle. He thought it was cool. He was instantly nicknamed 'Skateboard Head'.

Getting a good nickname can be a great help. A nickname can make you more familiar with your new teammates. A guy joined our club and said his name was 'Dolphin'. When I asked him why, he said 'cos I'm useless on land'. How could you not like him? And nobody minded when he came last in all the sprints.

A young lad joined our team from the underage ranks. He was seventeen, six foot two, with a beard. He will forever be known as 'The Man-Child'.

Some can't be explained. I was introduced to a new player called 'Minx'. I was looking at him side-eyed, thinking, 'What has he been getting up to at the weekends to earn him that name?' I never did find out. But I did tog off at the other side of the dressing room all the same.

If you don't have a nickname, make one up. Take matters into your own hands. You don't want a bad one. We had a coach, Mr Burns. His favourite pupil was christened 'Smithers' because he was always licking up to Mr Burns like the evil power tycoon in *The Simpsons*.

A guy who wore his black hair greased back was told he looked like a porn star and is now forever known as 'Fabio'.

There's no way you'd pick Fabio or Skateboard Head to play centre forward.

Your performance at the first two or three training sessions will determine how you're perceived for ever more. Try get into a drill with the good lads. It'll bring you on as a player and it's much better than being seen as part of the dossers. If you're hanging around with the lads known for drinking, they'll say the same about you.

Score a nice point in the first minute and they'll say you're talented. Break a hurley and they'll say you're tough. I recommend both. Because they all asked who this new Dolphin fella was, and we were able to reassure all the old lads, he's able to score points and he broke two hurleys off the full back. Wow, what a find!

WHO TO MARK AT TRAINING?

JB: You have two options.

Option one: mark a guy who they think is great. If you can do well on him, you're the hottest prospect since Xabi Alonso. Or it'll backfire and he'll absolutely roast you.

Option two: mark a fella who's no good. You can absolutely go to town on him, shoot at every opportunity and hope that they're blinded by the eight points you scored and neglect to notice you were marking a 45-year-old milkman who has two bad knees and is more awkward than a newborn calf. He only came down to get out of the house. You've burned him alive with your out-of-town skills. If it's football, be sure to shoot with the outside of your boot if you can. When auld lads see this, their heads explode.

THE FIRST MATCH

JS: It's important to lay down a marker when it comes to your debut for your new team. Championship is championship no matter where you're from or who you play for. When I made my debut for Cahir GAA, having just transferred clubs from my hometown Roscrea, I knew I had to make a statement. How did I make that statement? Everybody loves a good scrap, don't they?

I could sense my teammates were a little wary of me. I used a lot of hair gel back in those days, which immediately made me stand out. (Most of my new teammates had never brushed their hair, let alone gone through the beauty regime I was implementing to look my best for the championship.) I knew I had to endear myself to them and let them know that I was one of the guys now. Midway during the second half of my debut and with the game in the melting pot against our neighbours, Fethard, our captain and talisman, become involved in a scuffle with their full back, who's not to be trifled with.

Time to make that statement. The opposition's goalkeeper, who's a big man – well, that's putting it mildly, he's more of a sumo wrestler than a GAA goalie – makes a beeline for our captain. I intercept the goalkeeper's best efforts to decapitate our captain and manage to drag-wrestle him to the ground. I'm a fairly big unit myself and onlookers have described our tangle as looking at two overweight builders fighting over who gets the last breakfast roll in Spar on a Monday morning. The goalkeeper and me went at it hammer and tongs. Well, in truth it lasted about ten seconds, we were both wrecked. Myself, our captain, the giant goalie and the full back all get a yellow card following the scuffle. No one got hurt and we won the game.

Later that night when the whole team went out for a few celebratory pints, I'm cornered by our captain and a few of our more experienced players. 'Fair play for jumping into the scrap today, you're not a bad auld fella,' my captain mutters. I was thrilled, and so the nickname 'Smacks' was born.

That's how you make a fucking statement.

NEVER LET HER MAMMY WATCH

JS: Mickey, you also mentioned the love of a good woman brought you to the parish. It was a similar situation with me. This is normally considered a positive, but it wasn't a positive for me as my good woman at the time decided to bring her mother along to watch the game. It was a day I'll never forget, a league game on a Sunday morning. I mean, who puts on a league game of a Sunday morning? Sunday mornings are sacred. The only activity a young lad in his early twenties should be doing at that particular time of the week is munching on a jambon and drinking his bodyweight in Dioralyte to try and cure his hangover – I know this because it's exactly what I was doing that sunny Sunday morning right before I had to go and play this poxy league match.

The game started bad for me, I spotted a couple of sliothars as they rained in from midfield and was becoming more and more agitated as I fumbled one after another, watching on as my marker had a field day. Being agitated was also a by-product of the fifteen pints of Coors Light and copious amounts of shots floating around in my gut from last night's antics. Then I finally catch a ball, turn my marker and I'm dragged down for a stone-wall penalty. The referee doesn't give it. I'm like a dog, I'm thick enough from the drink and this referee has me at boiling point. Also, this same referee works as a barman in the pub I was boozing in the night before. Yes, he refused to serve me at 1.30 a.m. the night before, but it's the lack of a penalty I'm more pissed off about now. I begin a tirade of abuse aimed at the referee that

Roy Keane would have been proud of. (DISCLAIMER: insulting referees is something we don't condone, though they *can* be pricks.)

The referee had heard enough and marched towards me, chest puffed out, only too happy to show me a red card. He thought that was the end of it. *Wrong.* I walked off the pitch still ranting and raving and took my seat in the stand. A word to the wise, Mickey – be on your best behaviour if your future mammy-in-law is coming to watch your silky skills in action. That day I had to deal with a pissed-off partner and a pissed-off mammy and could no longer get pissed in my local as following my red card I was now barred by the referee / barman. Not my finest work.

SOCIALISE WITH YOUR NEW TEAMMATES

JB: In fairness, this is half the reason anyone plays sport.

In GAA it'll probably be the pub. The chances of a cornerback asking you if you fancy a spot of canoeing after training are slim. Our advice is to go with them. A few sociable jars is a great way to get to know your new teammates better. Our tips:

Don't be shy. If there's one thing worse than the Black and Tans, it's people who're no craic. You don't have to be on the table going Freddie Mercury, but you should contribute *something* or you could be left on the bench for the Sunday session.

Buy your round. Getting into a round with GAA lads is treacherous. Some can lower pints like water into a barrel of sawdust while others will nurse a beer all night, reminding you that there's a league match in six months' time that they want to be ready for. All the same, do your best. If there's one thing worse than people who're no craic, it's people who won't buy their round.

Get to know the auld lads. There'll probably be a GAA bar somewhere in the town, a safe zone free of Instagram and soccer players. Call in there and sit in with the lads. They'll educate you on your new club and tell you exactly where you're going wrong. You'll learn about the time each one of them roasted the great county player of their time, how many titles the club has, or should have, and all the things you have to live up to if you're to be as good as they were. This is all historical fact with absolutely no bias. Anyway, it's highly entertaining in short doses.

Be sure to buy them a pint too – they might be picking the team and you'd be surprised how creamy porter can get a lad from number 17 to number 15.

Mikey, you have a woman. That's why you're moving to this area. So it's important you don't get your head turned by all these strange women in the pub. If a beautiful woman walks past, be careful what you say, she may be someone's girlfriend of sister. If you're seen talking to her for more than fifteen seconds, in a small town that's enough for a rumour to start: 'He was seen with the young wan of the Delahuntys and he has a girlfriend. I hear he's some man for the women!'

LEND A HAND AT THE FIELD DAY

JB: A great way to become a part of your new club is to offer your services by being a volunteer at the annual field day. This might be the club's main source of income for the year and is taken very seriously, as you can imagine. The field day brings all the families in the parish together so it's the perfect opportunity to get to know everyone and they will in turn be thinking, 'Isn't he a great man getting involved and helping out and he not even here a wet week.' But beware – there's some work to be carried out and it's not pretty. Some jobs are better than others, but this guide should steer you in the right direction. In our experience from many's a Cahir GAA field day we've been slaving at – and we suspect all field days are run the same – the following three jobs are to be avoided at all costs:

1. THE QUAD TOUR

The quad tour is a glamorous name for what is essentially the club chairman (who of course is a farmer and has access to a quad) attaching a sheep trailer to his quad and ferrying kids of all ages around the GAA field. This is normally the main attraction at the field day. The problem is for the man or woman collecting the €2. The kids are hopped up on TK red lemonade and Skittles and it can be hard to keep control of them and get them into the pen. Yes, that's not a typo: they actually keep the kids in a sheep pen. I know you're probably wondering about health and safety here but if you've seen our club chairman driving the quad at breakneck speed up the side of our stand dragging a sheep trailer with forty juvenile players bobbing around in the back, then keeping the kids in a pen while they await this exhilarating experience is the least of our health-and-safety concerns. When asked about health-and-safety-procedures our club chairman released the following statement: 'The key is to pack the kids in tight enough into the trailer – that way, if we were to crash, they wouldn't even budge, let alone get hurt.'

2. THE MINIGOLF

Patrolling the minigolf can be tough, essentially because it's not *actually* minigolf. The aim of the game is to putt the golf ball through one of three holes that have been cut out of some leftover skirting board. It's impossible. And bear in mind that the putting surface you're using is also the goalmouth of our football pitch, which at times can be tough to play football on, never mind golf. If you do miraculously manage to get the ball through the skirting board you win the grand prize, which is a bottle of Score cola. It's a fairly shite prize when you consider a bottle of Score cola is 30 cent and it's 50 cent a shot at the minigolf. Avoid this job unless you enjoy a tongue-lashing from pissed-off parents who insist this is a rip-off. Of course, they're right – but hey, the club need to fundraise.

3. JUDGING THE BONNY BABY COMPETITION

Nobody – *nobody* – wants to be the one to tell Sheila who works in the local deli that her baby isn't the winner. We've been there and it's the reason we haven't had a jambon in over eight months. The bonny baby competition normally brings out all the yummy mummies in the parish ready to have their child declared the bonniest. And in a small parish things can get heated, so if you want to get to know people in your new club, make sure you're not the one telling them their kid isn't cute enough, like Big Barry Ryan from our club who told local publican Mary that her child resembled something out of *Lord of the Rings*. He hasn't been seen for a while ...

Avoid the committee at all costs.

JS: Inevitably, after a training session, when you're broken up from chasing fit young lads and farmers attempting to chop off your blow-in limbs, when you're at your least prepared and most vulnerable, a man in his sixties will grab you by the arm and in front of several other club stalwarts proclaim: 'What about you Doyle, here's a good man – you'll surely give a hand on the committee, won't you?' This is not a question. The approving nods and 'good man, Doyle' coming over his shoulder signal the danger you now find yourself in.

Before you know it, your Thursday nights will be spent debating the price of fencing and the ideal brand of lime to use when lining the field. (Having served on a committee, we can tell you white paint does the job too.) You do not need this. You want to be accepted into your new club, yes, but a committee that seems initially harmless may turn out to be a web from which you will *never* extricate yourself. These men have been proudly serving on this committee since the day they were snared forty years ago by the auld stagers in their time.

There are big decisions to be made in a club, important debates to be had, but you won't be making them. It takes a good twenty-five years before they'll start listening to you. Everyone under fifty is a young fella getting carried away. Suggest soup and sandwiches after training and you'll be reminded that 'we are not a charity' and the club treasurer is no relation to Mother Teresa.

Your job will be more along the lines of directing traffic at matches, armed with a high-vis vest and zero local knowledge, refereeing treacherous under-11 parish league matches and manning the score board when yer club is hosting games. This is all good work that has to be done in a club, but you, as a new man, need to concentrate on your on-field reputation and leave the arguing with disciplinary boards to the wily old foxes.

JB: Somehow, some way, you must escape it. 'I haven't time' has been tried by many. I recommend you go with something they won't expect. If the meetings are held in the dressing room, say you're allergic to the fluorescent lights and couldn't stay in there any longer than five minutes or you might break out into a terrible rash – it may even spread and affect the whole club! It would be in everyone's best interests if you didn't attend. This'll be met with nods of 'by God' and 'ya, I heard of a fella who had that alright' and 'ah mind yourself, Doyle'. Sorry I can't join, lads, I'd only love to!

If you've implemented this advice and you're still unsure as to your status within the club you might wanna take the following quiz. This should sort you right out:

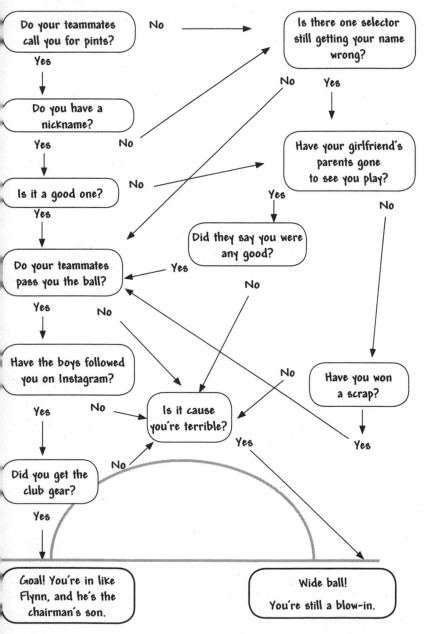

Dear Johnnies,

I need a blast of advice from ye two. I'm up to ninety as we say in Offaly. I took the plunge recently and finally moved out of home. I felt like it was time I cut the apron strings and got stuck into the big bad world. I must admit, though, I do pop home at least twice a week for a bit of dinner. No one cooks like your mammy, right? Anyway, my problem is this: I've moved in with a long-term friend of mine who I've known since we were in school and he is absolutely driving me insane. The man is, for want of a better word, a pig. Actually, having worked in a meat factory, pigs are cleaner, and I bet they keep their pens in a better condition than my mate keeps our house in. I thought it was gonna be class moving out with one of my buddies, but it's quickly turning into a nightmare. We live in a three-bedroom house and we're currently looking for someone to fill the third room. I guess I need some advice on how to get my friend to be a better housemate. Do I confront him? And what if we get another housemate who's just as bad? What are the telltale signs of a bad housemate? Would living with a girl be easier? I know you guys used to live together and yer still friends? Please help me with this before I contract some sort of bacterial infection from living with a man who's had a half-eaten pizza in his room for the past six weeks. Thanks in advance, lads!

Peter Cleary,
Co. Offaly

JS: Well, Peter, the first thing I would say is that you need to move away from Offaly. I'm only joking, I love Offaly really. Actually no, I don't, but I'm willing to put aside my beef with Offaly to help you out here. We'll get onto your friend shortly but for now let's talk about the imminent arrival of your new housemate on the scene.

PICKING HOUSEMATES IS NEVER EASY

JB: I'd advise picking a housemate who's a bit of a character, not just some bore who doesn't come out of his room from one end of the week to the other. I like having a housemate who's spontaneous, but obviously in a good way. I'm half cracked myself, which is handy. It gives me the ability to connect abstract concepts and ideas, which is great when creating our songs, sketches or podcasts. But I will never, never know how my old housemate's brain operated. He was a great man for the craic. He once said to me: 'Johnny B, you're into music and GAA. Some fellas are into cars or tractors. I'm into the craic.' He meant it, too. He was a craic connoisseur. A session aficionado. Knew everyone and everyone knew him and liked him. How could you not? A right man to have at a house party, as long as the party wasn't in your house.

One night I awoke to the strangest sound coming from downstairs. It was pure horror-film stuff. I grabbed a hurley and ran down to the kitchen in my jocks, expecting to flake the head off some Freddy Krueger-like intruder trying to rob our TV. There he was with a few friends after the pub, and what was making the noise? Our diesel lawnmower. Humming loudly in the middle of the kitchen, and he operating it. I looked at him, he looked at me, and then he said: 'I'm just trimming back the auld tiles, they were gone a bit wild.'

I had to laugh. What a line, I couldn't get mad, it was too much craic. I convinced him to turn off the lawnmower as the diesel fumes were becoming an issue. He said fair enough and we all sat down at the table while he explained his new-found interest in gardening.

I went back to bed, only to be re-awoken by the unmistakable sound of that lawnmower. Upon entering the kitchen, the lawnmower was turned over on its side. He'd taken the overflowing black bin bag out of the bin, tied it up and flung it into the spinning steel blade of the lawnmower. Garbage confetti showered around the room. 'Handier than Mr Binman,' he said.

That was the end of the party. The next day he cleaned up and the house remained reasonably unscathed, bar a slight hint of diesel. I found out later that a lad from Bansha had attempted to wash his adidas jacket in the dishwasher. (It actually worked ok.)

A few weeks later the landlord, Mick, called to collect his rent and give the place a look-over. He said: 'Lads, I have to tell ye, I got a noise complaint from the neighbours.' He didn't even believe the words himself as they came out his own mouth. 'Lads, did one of ye have a chainsaw or something going in the house one night?'

To which my craic-loving housemate replied, quick as a flash, 'Ah that's Johnny B and his auld boom-boom music.'

'Ye might keep it down in future, Johnny,' said Mick.

'No bother, Mick,' says I.

JS: I'd be avoiding that type of housemate like I'd avoid a drunk lad outside Coppers at four in the morning, roaring at the top of his lungs that 'Laois are on the up!' They're not, by the way. It's your first time living away from your parents, so you need a nice easy life. If you can manage to dodge the following housemates then you should be as happy as a farmer during silage season:

Type A: The cereal offender

JS: This housemate always has a bowl of cereal in their hands and no matter how many times you ask them to make sure and wash up, they never do. Now I don't know if you've ever tried to wash a bowl that's caked in Weetabix and been left to marinate in the sink for two weeks. It's a fucking impossible job. I reckon if they discovered Weetabix in the 1800s it would have been used to build castles because once it sets it basically becomes concrete.

I lived with one of my best friends from home in college. It was all going smoothly until the bowls in our flat started to go missing. I asked my friend about them and he shrugged it off, saying he only used plates, despite the fact the man lived on a diet of cereals and Pot Noodles. Now, I knew he was lying cos eating cereals on a plate is defying gravity. One morning I popped into his room to borrow some hair gel and there they were, all the bowls we'd ever owned thrown into a corner. Mould, old Pot Noodle – you name it and it was growing inside these bowls. It looked like a science experiment gone wrong. I was horrified. 'I'm not cleaning these,' I thought. Instead I pulled back the duvet and filled his bed with the toxic bowls and went about my business. Needless to say, there was never a dirty bowl found in the house again. Come to think of it he didn't change his sheets either.

Type B: The bin bandit

JS: An evil genius. If you're wondering why it always seems to be your job to empty the bins, then it's obvious – you're living with a bin bandit. I've seen their type in operation. When the bin is overflowing, they'll do everything in their power not to bring it out. If that means jumping from the roof into the bin just to squash it down two inches, they'll do it. I had a friend who prided himself on never having to empty the bin. He'd strategically place the rubbish on top of the bin until it resembled the Leaning Tower of Pisa. It basically became a game of Jenga, but instead of using wooden building blocks we were using kebab wrappers, used teabags and other such shite you'd find in the bin.

One night we decided enough was enough. We were sick of this rubbish-dodger, so when he went for his traditional Friday night pints, we took the bulging bags of rubbish (which he promised he'd dump) and stacked them on top of each other till they completely covered his bedroom door. We woke up the next morning expecting the bags to be gone but instead found our housemate fast asleep on top of the bags. In his own words, he'd lost the brain early and had the mother of all hangovers, so the rubbish would have to wait to be dumped until he recovered. He never learned his lesson – on both counts – but it's ironic he now works in a recycling plant. The rubbish literally caught up with him.

Type C: The house-party has-been

JS: A house party can be a great idea when all housemates are involved. It's not such a great idea if it's just one person constantly causing havoc. Sticky floors and half-finished cans left scattered around the sitting room on a Sunday morning along with half your GAA team sleeping off last night's antics will become the norm. If I sound like I'm speaking from experience here that's because I am, but I was always a team player when it came to house parties – unlike Davy, a man I used to live with.

When you've got work in SuperValu at 7 a.m. the last thing you want is to be woken at 3.30 a.m. to the sound of Scooter's 'Nessaja' blaring from the sitting room, but that's what happened. It sounded like there were twenty people bopping around my sitting room. I jumped out of bed and was on my way to confront everyone when I hear Davy shouting, 'Let's have a game of truth or dare!' I decide to wait at the door just to try and figure out who these nutters were. My housemate got no reply to his offer so I pounced, flinging open the door, ready to give him a tongue-lashing. I was expecting a room full of people but there's nobody in the room, only Davy. He was a strange man and to this day I'm convinced he was gearing up to play a full-blown game of truth or dare with himself. Thankfully he moved out the following week.

Type D: The 'I'll have the rent Monday' rogue

JS: In every house I've ever lived in there's always been one person who never has the rent on time. These housemates seem to be capable of spending a fortune on Jägerbombs and River Island skinny jeans but are unable to produce the money for rent. I'm ashamed to say that when Johnny B and myself used to live together back in our younger years, I was a nightmare at paying rent. Johnny B was generally a lot cleverer than me. If I got my runners dirty, I'd consider buying a new pair. Johnny B, on the other hand, had a pair of Sambas so old they could nearly draw a pension. One Saturday after one of my shopping hauls I arrive into our sitting room to find the coffee table and floor covered in old newspapers. Perhaps Johnny B was in a spot of bother, trying to dispose of a body? He wasn't. What he was attempting was much worse. He swanned into the room with his Sambas under his arm, a paintbrush in one hand and an industrial-sized tin of Dulux in the other. I thought that maybe he was going to paint our gable end, but I was wrong. Johnny B sat at the coffee table and when questioned about what he was doing, told me he was 'painting the soles of his Sambas white to make them look good as new'. I shit you not. I slagged him, saying, 'Are you gonna paint the adidas lines white too as well?' He thought this was a great idea and proceeded to do exactly that. It's remarkable to think that just last week Johnny B climbed Croagh Patrick wearing those exact Sambas. Fame will never go to his head.

Type E: The sloth

JS: This wild beast can be found skulking around the sitting room normally wearing just a pair of boxers. Most 'house sloths' spend more time watching reruns of daytime television shows than worrying about their own personal hygiene. I know about these types, I've come across them before. I lived with a sloth in college. Well, when I say college, this guy never actually went to college. He would sit in the sitting room all day long, surviving solely on a diet of Custard Creams and Bacon Grills, both of which have the nutritional value of a cardboard box. This guy had an unhealthy relationship with the Xbox console, which is a common trait in most house sloths. On one occasion we were convinced he'd ditched college and returned to Carlow, where he was from. Four days had passed and we hadn't heard from him. He's definitely gone back to Carlow, right? Wrong. After four long days, the sloth emerges from his room. Two red eyes on him like two pool balls. He walks into the kitchen, where the rest of us are perched at the table having our dinner.

'Where've you been?' we asked. Proud as punch he declares he's just completed *Call of Duty: Black Ops*. Four days he'd been in that room playing the console and hadn't left once. To this day we don't know how he survived, or how he went to the toilet. Wait … oh … that explains the smell when he left.

ROUTINE IS KEY

JB: Having a routine is the key to having a happy house. Introducing a cooking rota is also a genius move. It's helpful to build a bit of team spirit in the house with everyone feeling they contribute their own little bit and it can also be a good way to save time and dishes. That's the real beauty of it. I lived with two other lads for a while and we shared Tuesdays, Wednesdays and Thursdays. Tuesday was my day and I always tried to cook something good. My mam had given me enough of a culinary education to survive in the world. One of our housemates, though, had not been as educated, which led to his fascination with pasta bakes. At first, I didn't notice but after six months I had to ask, 'Man, have you been cooking a pasta bake every Thursday since Christmas?' What a weird dish to specialise in. It's like he'd read the first page of a cookbook and thought, 'That's the one.'

When you're house-sharing, one thing you've got to do is leave your feelings at the front door. Don't be one of these people who is easily offended. Smacks and I had a housemate who put red sauce on *everything*! One day Smacks cooked a curry and yer man, without even tasting it, goes straight for the red sauce.

'If you put red sauce on that curry I'll throw you out the window.'

Silence. *Squeeezzze.* A quarter-bottle of ketchup goes into the chicken curry. He mopped it up. Loved it. Good thing too, cos Smacks never cooked for him again. If he was ever stuck for a snack, he had his favourite: crackers and red sauce, a can of Lucozade to wash it down. I don't think he'll be releasing a range of fitness DVDs anytime soon and I think he has a heart condition now, but anyway …

To be fair, if you don't have any basic skills around the house, that shouldn't stop you from moving out of home. There's a way around everything nowadays. I lived with one guy who used only disposable plates and cutlery, not because we had none in the house but because he was allergic to cleaning. One meal, then straight in the bin. Madness. The fella hated washing clothes so much, he brought everything to the dry cleaners. He'd never learned how to iron at home and wasn't gonna start now. He's actually going out with the girl who runs the local launderette. Needs must.

Peter, I know you're struggling to get your 'pig' of a housemate to clean up. Don't keep nagging him, just trick him into it. This'll work a treat for you and he'll be none the wiser. So, here's how: I had a lucky feeling one Friday evening, so I bought €10-worth of Euromillions tickets. The rota said it was my turn to clean the oven. What a horrible job. I made a deal with my housemate: if he cleaned the oven and I won the Euromillions, I'd give him half. Thirty-five million to clean the oven. Didn't win the millions, but Joey had the oven shining.

One thing you should always remember is this: inviting people over to your house always seems like a great idea at the time, but beware of the consequences, especially when beer is involved. I know what you're thinking: 'Ah they're my friends, it'll be grand.' Your friends are the worst culprits. Trust me. A slightly older friend had moved to Dublin and was living in a flat near the quays with his lovely girlfriend. She was heading home for a weekend, so he invited us up. Telling young Tipperary men that there's free accommodation going in the Big Smoke for the weekend was like winning a trip to the moon. So up we went. All thirteen of us in a one-bedroom flat.

The Chernobyl-like smell of feet and pizza could be cleaned, but putting that many lads in an apartment can put your gaff in serious jeopardy.

One of our friends was particularly fond of Jameson whiskey, so he hid a bottle in the apartment for when he came home from the pub – we think ahead in Tipperary. There weren't many places to hide it, so he reached in and put it on top of the water tank. After returning from the pub he realised that this was Dublin and that this apartment had been built during the boom. The water tank had no cover on it and the bottle had dropped straight to the bottom of the four-foot-deep tank. We came home to find him with a steak knife in his hand, about to cut a hole in the bottom of the tank. This would have retrieved the bottle but would have turned the apartment into Aqua Dome. Harmless fun, he said, but you can see how it nearly got out of hand.

JS: Now back to your 'pig' of a housemate. He's your friend, so let's try resolve this. Ask him nicely to pull himself together. Tell him you brought a girl over and she said the smell from his room is disgusting and he'll never find a girlfriend if he doesn't cop on. Trust me, this will work. It worked when I did it to Johnny B.

JB: It was the other way around if my memory serves me right.

JS: If this doesn't work, then it's time to play a few pranks on him until he learns his lesson. The best one I've seen executed was from my college days when we had a house outing to to see the horror film *Paranormal Activity*. Our friend Roger had a great talent for leaving every electrical appliance in the gaff on – this resulted in sky-high bills, not ideal for struggling students. But Roger scares easily, and we knew it. Time to teach him a lesson. Andy, who's the smallest, rose to the challenge. He cut a hole in the lining under Roger's mattress and managed somehow to get inside it. Half an hour later, Roger eventually went to bed. Cue the screams. Andy, scraping Roger's bedframe, whispers, '*Turn off all plugs ... the electricity bill is too high ...*'

Roger took the prank well and the electricity bill for the next quarter was halved. All's well that ends well.

You mentioned you might prefer to live with a girl. I bet you think she'll be like another mammy, don't ya? It won't happen. Living with women is no cakewalk. Take these following points on board if you're going to take the plunge.

1. Your electricity bill will go up: straighteners, curlers, wands and rollers all have to be used, and that's only on their hair.

2. Fake-tan smells: most girls I've lived with are layered in tan at least once a week. So unless you like the smell of gone-off biscuits, this can be a problem.

3. They'll bring boyfriends over. And they'll more often than not be dickheads. One guy who was going out with an ex-housemate of mine insisted on turning on the hairdryer while doing the deed with his lady. I mean, we don't wanna keep harping on about the electricity but ...

4. You'll have to get up an hour earlier. If you like something as simple as brushing your teeth in the morning, you'll have to beat her to it. Once she gets in that bathroom there's no getting her out.

5. You'll have to watch *Say Yes to the Dress*. There's no way around it. If a girl moves in, she'll be the boss of everything, including the TV. Just accept it. Eventually you'll get to like the programme.

JS: Peter, to conclude, the best bit of advice we can give you is move out of Offaly altogether.

JB: Ah Smacks, give him a break.

GOING TO

COLLEGE

Dear Johnnies,

Hello, hello, hello, as ye say yourselves. I'm taking a break from attempting to study because I'm looking for a bit of help from ye two bucks. I'm currently in my Leaving Cert year and haven't a clue what I want to do. I think I want to go to college because I don't really know what else is out there for me. All my cousins are in college and they seem to be having some craic. My parents want me to get an education. What do you lads think? Should I go to college? What other options are out there in Ireland? I have a part-time job at the weekends and I don't wanna do that for ever! I'd love to get yer expert opinions on things.

Chips, cans and John Mullane,

Fionn

Co. Waterford

JB: Firstly, Fionn, we're not experts. I mean, we tell jokes for a living, so career advice wouldn't be our strong point, but we don't let that deter us. The good thing is you've got time on your side. When we were in Leaving Cert year, we still thought we were gonna be professional soccer players and rock stars.

JS: This is genuinely true: when I was in Transition Year I visited the career-guidance teacher. She asked me what I wanted to do with my life. I replied like a shot, 'A professional footballer, miss.' She soon pointed out I had a dodgy knee, was carrying a few pounds from my chicken-roll addiction and didn't stand a chance of making it as a soccer player. I then set my sights on playing county. Unfortunately, that doesn't get you an honours degree or pay the bills.

Given the fact that you mentioned you were attempting to study leads us to believe you might be capable of qualifying to get into college. We had a friend who drank more pints than he got Leaving Cert points. You seem to have your head screwed on and know that to get an education you need to do some form of study. We wish we'd known that when we were sitting exams.

We regret not properly giving the whole college thing a go.

We recommend you go down the college route but you've got lots of different roads you can go down, young man. Everybody is different and, as an auld lad down our clubhouse says, 'No point being a farmer if you don't like the smell of shite.'

Fionn, here're your options if you choose not to go to college.

GET AN APPRENTICESHIP

JB: Last year 13,000 young people in Ireland opted for an apprenticeship over college. Why? Well as soon as you start, you get paid. It's not Snoop Dogg money, but it's enough to buy an Opel Corsa and ten pints of Heineken every week. While students will be surviving on Pot Noodle and vodka, you'll be feasting on breakfast rolls and chicken rolls and ham-and-cheese rolls. You'll be eating a lot of rolls, basically. Because you'll be on the go, actually working. The first year of college is handy out – go to the odd lecture, make a few female friends, etc. As a first-year apprentice, you will be dogged to do every dirty job going.

I was made to chisel parts out of walls with a hammer and stone chisel. There was a big electric jackhammer in the van, but I didn't know that and the older lads thought it was gas craic to watch me bust my ass hammering. The job moved a lot slower cos of it, like it actually cost the boss money, but he considered it worth it, just to watch me sweat. It definitely toughens you up.

If you don't like dirt, then the building site is not for you, Fionn. If you get a bad boss, you could be in for some grilling. You want to learn how to be a carpenter and erect roofs? You could be mixing cement and carrying slates for the first six months.

If you think working outside with your hands sounds nice, you're wrong. Have you ever been outside? It's Ireland. It rains a lot, and you'll be working in all kind of conditions, in all kind of places.

There's also a complete lack of ladies. Only 1 per cent of people doing apprenticeships are women. The only bit of arse you'll see will be when Big Frank bends down to plaster the bottom of a wall. Plasterers seem to just refuse to tuck in their T-shirts. Christ, lads, will ye tuck it in? I'm scarred for life.

The best thing about doing an apprenticeship is the craic you'll have. It's tough, it's hard work, your hands will be like sandpaper, you may have to use those Portaloos on building sites that are straight out of Hiroshima, but it's all lads in the same boat, all together. The slagging will be savage, but you'll laugh your ass off.

When we were in school, everybody said, 'If you do a trade, at least you'll always have work.' Then BANG – the recession hit and 300,000 young people emigrated. Dropped their tools and walked off site. There must be some fella who went around collecting them tools and has now made a fortune. Trades can also be hard on the body. Many tradesmen start on the tools but by forty they've retrained and are now overseeing the job, getting the young fellas to do the donkey work. Proper order. No point having a dog and barking yourself.

On my first day I was told to report to their head offices in Clonmel. So in I go, in my good clothes, expecting some safety training and to sign a bit of paperwork. An hour later I was hacking out old windows in a housing estate, covered in dust. And to top off a nightmare first day I got white silicone on my good blue jumper. Heartbreaking. I'd only had that jumper a week.

As a tradesman, it's imperative you get a good pair of boots. If a man turns up in a cheap pair, no one on site will respect him. A good pair of safety steel-toecap boots says you're here to do work, manly work. The

Snickers pants with all the pockets is for the real trade enthusiast, who's carrying four types of pencil, just in case.

An apprenticeship includes three stints in the classroom. Here you're supposed to learn the theory behind what you've been applying on site. Your first trip to the classroom is twenty weeks long. My first stint in the classroom was in the FÁS training centre in Kilcohan Industrial Estate, Co. Waterford – an absolute holiday camp compared to the building site. This phase happens early in your apprenticeship so no one has dropped out yet, meaning every lunatic who didn't get into college and every useless article who can't drive a nail is probably still in the course. Lads who were so uncoordinated, their bosses made them dig holes and wash buckets when they should have been fitting stairs. They're now all in your class, and they have sharp tools. Some guys are really talented. They will fly through the information. Other guys would rather eat the pages than complete the drawings. You get into a trade, maybe because you did a bit on your summer holidays and thought, 'These lads have some craic and make good money,' never thinking you'd have a scientific calculator and a T-square on your desk. To get a higher credit on all seven phases of your apprenticeship actually takes brains and hard work. Whether you get a pass or an honours, though, doesn't matter a shite, no one will ever look at it. Can you do the job? Grand, after that, just don't be the guy with the hammer and stone chisel.

GET A FULL-TIME JOB

JS: If there's one thing I hate more than Offaly, then it's having a proper job. I recommend you get a really shitty full-time job before you decide to go to college. That way, when you do eventually go to college you'll see how easy that is compared to full-time work.

I of course did this the wrong way around. I went to college first and flunked out, thinking that getting a job didn't seem like such a tough prospect. How fucking wrong was I? I managed to secure a job in my local bacon factory in Roscrea and it was grim. My mam would drop me to the factory each morning at 7 a.m. and I'm not ashamed to say that as a nineteen-year-old man, I cried on the commute on several occasions. It was that bad. I felt like a toddler in baby infants being dropped to school on their first day. As soon as I arrived, we'd all queue up to get our white pants and protective jacket. It was like a scene from *The Shawshank*

Redemption. You'd swear we were on death row. We'd be given our uniform from an old man who'd try and brighten your day with a joke. Easy for him to joke, he was near retirement. In my eyes I had another forty-six years of this. I used to work beside a Polish man called Victor who I'm fairly sure the factory grew. He was around four feet tall and didn't have a lick of English. I mean, not a drop. He was a lovely fella though. I'd try out some stand-up for him some days and in fairness to him he never complained, he just smiled and gave a thumbs up. The fact he couldn't understand me probably helped. That factory was a strange place. I'd just gone from school to college and now to this place. In school you'd almost be taking the piss out of people doing LCA, but in this place they were the bosses. For anyone reading this book who doesn't know what LCA is, that's where you do your Leaving Cert using crayons. I hope you take this horror story on board. If you decide to go down the route of getting a full-time job, don't take a job in a bacon factory.

TAKE A YEAR OUT ➡

JB: The gap year is a big deal for our good friends in tan land. It's basically an opportunity for the middle-

and upper-class school-leavers to dodge real work for a year. They normally travel the world exploring their sexuality and trying to find themselves while sharing a hostel in Thailand with a busload of pissed Brazilians. Imagine trying to justify a gap year to an Irish father – he'd have you in a full-time job as quick as you could pull a pair of skinny jeans up over your arse. I don't think us Irish could deal with taking a year of getting pissed and enjoying life while figuring out your next move. We'd never go back to normal life and end up on the strip trying to get tourists into some backstreet boozer for happy hour. If you've ever wondered how those middle-aged Irish men who're mahogany and wrinkled from the sun got that type of job, it's because they went on a gap year thirty years ago and are still on it. So, unless you want to shame your father down the local and hitchhike around Cambodia for fun, we suggest you avoid taking a year out as much as we avoid a night out in Carlow. Unless, of course, sitting around a campfire singing 'Kum ba yah' with a bunch of hippies who haven't showered since the last time Mike Denver's bleached hair was considered cool is your thing. That was a long, long time ago.

TAKE A PLC OR NIGHT COURSE

JB: I think a course like this is genius – it allows you to dip your toe into third-level education. Doing a course like this can give you a taste of college without forcing your poor parents to remortgage their house so you can go and piss their hard-earned savings up against a wall.

JS: I rushed into college because I just wanted to party and get out of home; I wasn't worried about studying and exams. I'm sure there are lots of secondary schools in your area providing a chance to enrol in a PLC course. Think of the advantages: you get to live at home and have Mammy fuss over you, hoover your room and serve up home-made dinners every day. Another positive is that you can go back to your old secondary school and chat up your English teacher. I mean, you're not technically her student any more so it's not inappropriate, is it?

JB: I think that's just you, Smacks.

JS: I still reckons she fancies me – that's half the reason I'm writing this book in an effort to impress her and tell her I'm an author now.

JB: Anyways, Fionn, we don't want you to make the same mistakes as us. We want you to give college a proper lash (two hands on the hurley and pull hard), but only if you follow this expert plan to a T.

JS: I couldn't get an expert.

JB: What'll we do so?

JS: Be grand. Sure, I know everything there is to know about college. I gave it a right go.

JB: Going out four nights a week and completing *Grand Theft Auto San Andreas* isn't exactly giving it a go.

JS: Relax! I've got this.

JOHNNY SMACKS'S TOP TIPS FOR SURVIVING COLLEGE

Commit to living there

Fifty per cent of the reason people want to go to college is to 'get loose'. I've never heard anyone say, 'Aw, I can't wait to go to college and study every evening.' Although I did say that to my parents. It didn't work. The other

50 per cent just want to get out of the clutches of Mammy and Daddy. They're dead right too. I feel that in order to fully get the college experience you need to live there – throw off the shackles and really discover yourself. Living at home may be a cheaper and handier alternative, but you can't pump out scooter tunes at four in the morning and confess your undying love for a fellow student with your parents in the next room. It's time to cut the apron strings and stand on your own two feet. You're a big boy now, Fionn. (PS Don't cut the apron strings completely – your parents are probably going to be funding this adventure.)

Stock up on shopping

If you're like me, Fionn, and are relying on your parents to give ya a few quid to keep ya fed for the week, here's an even better way. Get your mam to do the grocery shopping for you before you make your trip back to college on a Sunday. She'll know exactly what to get. I used to head back to Waterford with two industrial-sized shopping bags full to the brim of the good stuff – none of that own-brand shite. It's a win-win because you're not asking your mam directly for a handout, and she's happy in the knowledge that you're off to get an education and won't die of malnutrition. My mam was too busy to do my shopping one week so she just gave me the money instead. I bought two T-shirts from River Island. I looked class but I was fucking starving.

Actually attend college

Believe it or not, in order to obtain a degree, you must actually attend college. I wish I'd known this back in 2009. The Boomtown Rats had a song called 'I don't like Mondays'. Mondays were actually ok for me – it was Thursdays I couldn't handle. I must admit now that in my one year of second-level education I never, ever attended on a Thursday (Ma, I'm sorry if you're reading this), since Wednesday was the big student night out in Waterford. My housemate at the time (who shall remain nameless) informed me after his first day that college wasn't for him. I told him to give it time, that he was only after a few classes. He then told me he didn't actually go to any classes: he sat through ten minutes of an induction and left. In those ten minutes he'd realised he'd rather spend the rest of his college year living off his grant, sitting in nothing but a pair of boxer shorts while trying to complete *Metal Gear Solid* on the PlayStation. Each to their own, I guess.

Don't be a couch potato

Eating and drinking anything that makes financial sense is not the basis of a healthy diet, although I thought that a good balanced diet meant being able to walk home straight after a night out. Make sure to maintain some form of an exercise regime in college (dancing in a nightclub doesn't count). Beware of the freshers' stone – it's real, it's not a myth, and we've seen it first-hand. A lad on our GAA team, our top athlete, went away to college to study heath and exercise but when he returned at Christmas, he looked like a fella who hadn't done one minute of health and exercise. He was as fit as a greyhound leaving but resembled a sausage dog when he returned. The story goes that he moved into an apartment over an Italian restaurant, hence the nickname 'Pizza', as he's still affectionately known.

Always go home at weekends

Going home at weekends is the key to a happy college experience. A full belly, a blazing open fire and freshly washed and ironed clothes are not something you'll be familiar with from Monday to Friday as a struggling student. Make the most of these home comforts for the forty-eight hours you're there. Be like a squirrel

– they stock up on food and necessities because they know there are tough times ahead. It's no different for students, except that the tough times ahead are probably in the shape of Rag Week or whatever other gimmick you can use as an excuse for a week-long piss-up. Also, it's a good opportunity to hang out with your friends from home and tell them what a ladies' man you've turned into. Or is that just me? Ah … awkward.

Be clever with your finances

Being economical with your money is the key to college life. Let's face it, you don't want to be spending money on essentials like food and electricity. You wanna spend it on fun things like Malibu and bottles of Miller. I had a foolproof way of saving a few euro with a hearty breakfast almost for free. Do the maths: a plate of beans in the college canteen costs 40 cent. A full Irish is €4.40. Simply cover the contents of the full Irish with a mountain of beans so it looks like you're just getting a plate of them. You're basically making money. This obviously doesn't work well, Fionn, if you don't like beans. Also, any financial advice you take is from a man who once spent his weekly college budget on getting a tattoo. The tattoo was also spelt wrong. Seriously.

Don't blow the grant

The grant is as precious as Pot Noodle. For some students, it's the difference between the expensive vodka or the paint-stripper that's available for half nothing down the local off-licence. I lived with a fella in college – let's call him 'Randy' – who, unlike me, was eligible for the grant. Three months of college had passed and still no sign of Randy's grant arriving in his bank account. The good friend I was, I cooked him the odd dinner here and there and shared my cans of Dutch Gold with him at parties so as he didn't have to go without a night out due to the pending grant. God forbid he'd miss a night on the tiles. Then one Wednesday morning he bursts into the shack we were renting. 'Get your coat, the grant arrived.' I hadn't seen him this happy since Hillbilly's introduced a student meal deal for €4. I duly obliged, put my coat on and off we went. Randy said thanks a million for helping him out for the last few weeks. He wanted to treat me the only way he knew how. He took me to the local college bar in WIT, the Dome, where he treated me to breakfast, lunch and dinner. All of these meals were preceeded and washed down with a feed of pints. That day went from strength to strength and into the next day too. I eventually managed to get Randy back to our apartment, although it wasn't without the help of a shopping trolley I borrowed from the local Tesco. Champagne lifestyle on Coca-Cola wages. We both woke up with heads like busted couches the next morning but thankfully I hadn't spent half my grant in one day, unlike poor Randy.

Befriend the mature students

If there's anything you need to know, from timetables to bus routes, ask the mature students because they know everything. They'll also know who you shifted at 4 a.m. the night before. I mean, how was I to know that girl's mam was in my course? If you're not sure how to recognise these people, they'll be the group sitting in the first row constantly asking questions with freakishly colour-coded notebooks. They're super-organised. They've fucked up before, it's not going to happen again. When it comes to group projects, which are part and parcel of third-level education, immediately seek out a mature student to join your group. Always try and pull your weight in these group environments because if you don't, you'll be blacklisted. Don't ignore your group's texts and phone calls for days, and don't take the battery out of your phone to make sure there's no way in hell they could possibly contact you. Wow, I did really mess up college, but I feel like this is like a form of therapy for me. Fionn, pull your weight. To this day I can't go into TK Maxx in Waterford as I'm dodging a mature student I let down on a group project. Mary, if you're reading this, I'm sorry.

JB: Fionn, we wish you all the best as you set out on your path in life. Work hard, keep the head down and as Margaret in the Shamrock Lounge says: 'What's for ya won't pass you by.'

JS: And if that didn't work, just start making sketches and songs and uploading them online and cross your fingers and toes and hope that maybe one day that can be your full-time job. It worked out ok for us.

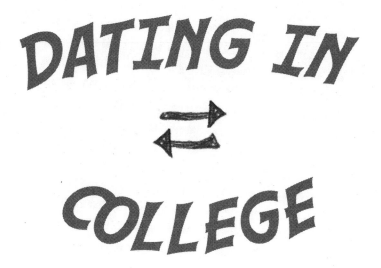

Dear Johnnies,

My name is Sarah. I'm from the green and red of Mayo. I'm heading to UL shortly to study agricultural science as well as hopefully meeting Mr Right. I've not had much luck with my love life in the past but I'm hoping ye can change that. I'm new to the dating scene as I'm quite a shy girl. I guess you could say I'm a late bloomer, but I'm ready to change all that. I'm hoping to find my very own Mr Right, who will have to be a decent guy that I can bring home to Daddy (who, bear in mind, is a tough farmer) and he's got to be a fella who won't mess me around. I've had my heart broken enough by Mayo losing so many All-Ireland finals. I need your advice because I wouldn't know where to start. I really don't know what to expect. Hopefully you guys can be my Cupid.

Thank you,

Sarah

Co. Mayo

JS: Sarah, your wish is our command.

JB: A late bloomer doing ag science. Maybe Daddy has had her working flat out on the farm at home, chasing cows, with no time for chasing boys.

JS: Well, I have some college experience, *and* some dating experience.

JB: Weren't you only in college a few weeks?

JS: Yeah, but I got the experience.

JB: You've had more failed relationships than a character in *EastEnders*.

JS: This is about Sarah, not me.

JB: Sarah, there's five different types of lads you're going to encounter when you get stuck into college life. We've rated them out of five for you and the readers of this book:

The quiet lad

Shoe-starers, as we call them. He'll be standing in the corner awkwardly staring at his shoes. He's got a heart of gold, but you'll have to break down the Berlin Wall, in this case his emotional barriers, in order to get a bit of conversation out of him. This beast should be approached subtly as he's easily startled outside of his natural habitat (most likely the study hall). He too may be a late bloomer and is not to be ruled out. Make an effort to talk to him, but if after two minutes he's proving to be too much work, then back away. As a farmer's daughter you already have loads of work on your plate, you don't need this guy draining your resources.

Suitability rating: 3/5

The GAA jock

Our GAA jock can be easily spotted as he's always sporting his skinny tracksuit pants, O'Neill's jersey and championship haircut. He has that confident walk attained from playing county minor and attending several debs. He'd be committed. Well, he'd be committed to training, and to you when he's not stretching his enormous quads. He'll be in good physical nick, which women like, we think. (Neither of us would know, cos we're not.) Don't let his enlarged pectoral muscles distract you from your course or your dating objectives. You've got to watch the bicep-to-brain ratio.

We advise you to let him approach you – and don't worry, he will. Then just ignore him. He'll come back for more. He may mistake you for a Jersey Puller. These do exist.

The Jersey Puller approach is effective in the short term, but it's not a good look and we don't recommend it for you, Sarah.

Suitability rating: 2/5   ➡️

The Flash Harry

This Richie Rich-looking lad didn't get into Trinity, but says he's transferring there next year. You'll smell this lad before you see him. His Hugo Boss aftershave will tingle your spidie senses. (There's surely one lad in Mayo wearing aftershave.) Flash Harry will leave a trail of destruction and broken hearts in his wake. This Hollister-wearing scarf-lover is put together like a ransom note. He enters college with not as much as a hair out of place. This guy looks like he sleeps standing up. We highly doubt he'll be any use to you back on the farm in Mayo. Dubarrys and slatted sheds don't make for a good combination.

This type of character is known to wine, dine and two-time unsuspecting females. He'll suck you in like a Dyson, with his charm, incredible jaw structure and being the only guy able to afford chinos and hair conditioner.

Most lads in UL will look like they're on their way back from a weekend in Electric Picnic. Here's a pearl of wisdom: if it's too good to be true, it probably is. Be wary of any lad who has money in college. A character like Flash Harry is to be avoided at all costs.

Unless we've got this totally wrong. It's highly possible. Maybe he's a nice guy. I mean, we're comedians, not experts.

Suitability rating: 1/5 ➡️

The rocker

This also includes crusties (you know, those people who never wash and live off the land and look like Galway people), goths, hoodies and stoners, aka 'corn dudes'.

There'll probably be a bunch of lads in your college studying sound engineering, but what they really want to study is being a rock star, though obviously this isn't a course – If it was, we'd both be enrolled by now. Always keep in mind you'll never find a corn dude on their own. They travel in packs, like penguins.

They may be wearing a hoodie with their favourite band on it – Sum 41, Nirvana or some new act that sounds like the name of a car part. 'Ya, Sump Pump are very cool, you probably wouldn't have heard of them.'

You might not actually find this guy on campus. He's most likely set up camp in your classmate's sitting room. Armed with a packet of Tuc biscuits, body odour, John Player Blue, headphones and of course *Resident Evil* on the PlayStation. The corn dude doesn't get to class much but swears he'll get the notes online and is well able for the course (he isn't – he's just there to pick up the grant). He may seem cool, but don't be fooled – he's not the guy for you, unless you fancy driving him to his Saturday job as a roadie for a Green Day tribute band in Nenagh. He's not a bad guy and we're sure he'll make some lady very happy someday, but his lack of farm knowledge and aversion to daylight could be a deal-breaker.

If you're up for a challenge, then he's the man for you.

Suitability rating: 2/5

The tang/country man

The tang is an affectionate term given to someone from the country, who's normally found sporting suede tan shoes, a Scania jacket, bootcut jeans and who owns a selection of check shirts. (That's the male tang now, although you wouldn't know sometimes.)

Statistically there should be 45 to 49 per cent tangs in your class. If it is too warm for the Scania jacket, look out for a pencil behind the ear – that's the symbol of the native tang. Their ringtone may be Nathan Carter's 'Wagon

Wheel' or 'Hit the Diff' by Marty Mone.

In terms of dating a tang, there's no two ways about it, you have to be able to jive. They say you can tell a lot about a man by the way he dances. Most tangs are like my old Berlingo van – hard to start, but then goes all night and also requires a lot of servicing.

He may not be the most romantic – a date could be a night out in the Stables bar in UL or a Mike Denver concert. He's not afraid of work, and is probably only in college to get out of Carlow, broaden his horizons and have the craic. We think Daddy would approve of the tang. He'll foot turf like a bastard. He'd outwork Flash Harry's whole family. He's as loyal as a sheepdog bitch. (Smacks is speaking from experience: he actually had a sheepdog and it *was* very loyal.)

Sarah, if this man sounds like your knight in shining armour, you may already *be* a tang!

Suitability rating: 4/5

←

JS: I know it's college, but we recommend trying to meet people sober. A hard thing to do.

JB: One place you should keep an eye out for is the canteen. I didn't get to chat to many girls in school. Myself and my mate Gonzo brought our own sandwiches. We were the only two people in Sixth Year to do it. Apparently, it's not cool. I don't care what anyone says, you can't bate a good ham sandwich, maybe with a bit of cheese on a Friday. The only lady we chatted up was the woman who controlled the soups, which were chicken and mushroom. The mushroom one was cat – the scabby First Years could have that muck. We had to sweet-talk the soup lady so she'd keep us two cups of chicken soup. Every day we skipped the queue, collected our chicken plunder (we never paid – don't try this in college, in fact don't try this in life) and sat in the canteen with the First Years all keeping a wide berth around us. Gonzo was hardcore and drove a motorbike. I think they were afraid of him. Sure I could have spent my lunchtimes chatting up girls, but there was chicken soup to be got in the canteen. So no, I never chatted up a girl on lunch! But if you see a nice-looking guy, watch how he treats the staff. If he's rude with the person giving him spuds, then he'll be rude to anyone and is to be avoided. It's also an opportunity to see if he's tight – some lads hide a black pudding under the beans (not mentioning any names here).

JS: Also keep an eye on his eating habits, if he's gulping it down, mouth open like Popeye eating spinach, he's not the man for you. If you can't spend five minutes across the table from him at lunchtime, you won't be spending the rest of your life with him.

JB: Don't be afraid to ask a guy out – it doesn't always have to be the man who makes the first move, but make him do some of the work by saying like, 'Are you gonna ask me out or what?' He will! Then you have your date, but there's still room for him to bring his A-game and impress you.

JS: You should always bring your A-game when it comes to any date, not just a first date. I've learned my lesson the hard way. I've been there, done that and fucked it up. I'm not the most romantic of people. Valentine's Day was fast approaching and I was in college at the time, on a diet of Pot Noodle and Bière d'Or (which resembled a cough bottle and had the same effect when drunk in bulk, to be fair). I'd been with this girl around a month and needed to take her somewhere for a meal as I'd given it the big man, saying, 'Ah, I'll take ya out somewhere nice, no bother.'

There was a bother, though. I was stone broke. I'm thinking, it has to be somewhere close by. I'm not paying for a taxi. Somewhere that serves quick, too – I'm meeting the lads for pre-drinks in an hour and I don't wanna be playing catch-up. Somewhere that isn't too lovey-dovey – don't want this girl thinking I'm in love with her.

And then it hit me, like a wrap of an elbow from a hairy Junior B full back: three letters, KFC. After sharing a boneless banquet and expressing how well this date went to the lads later that night, claiming I was some sort of love guru, she ended our relationship the next morning.

JB: You think that's bad. I once took a girl on a date to Tesco. It just kind of happened. It's not like I rang my favourite restaurant and they were booked up and I thought, ah you know where's class … the supermarket! We drove into town and walked around the shop, chatting. She showed me her favourite detergent; I showed her my favourite cheap cans. Got a little awkward as we walked past the condoms – I didn't realise they had such a selection of lubricants. She couldn't get out of that aisle quick enough. Down into the baby food and nappies. I couldn't get out of *that* aisle fast enough. They sold clothes down the back. We tried on hats. She had a good head for hats. I looked like Miley from *Glenroe*. It was late and the shop was very quiet, actually quite romantic, I thought. We bought ice cream and ate it in my van, watching the world go by. Beautiful. I forgot to buy spoons, so we had to use a ruler I had in my toolbox. We stopped seeing each other shortly afterwards. I never went back to Tesco.

JS: Wow, Johnny B, you're such a catch!

Sarah, you should always look for a guy who is sensitive, like me. Let's just hope he's not as sensitive as I was when I went on one of my first-ever dates with this girl from my class. I guess you could call it a second date, as our first rendezvous was in Harvey's nightclub in Waterford. As Justin Bieber boomed over the speakers, we were slumped in the shifting position, locking jaws. She was miming the words as we canoodled (I have to watch what I say – my poor mother will be reading this). This girl even knew the rap verse of 'Baby', featuring Ludacris. Love at first sight.

I suggested we go to the cinema during the week. I was the perfect gentleman, walked to meet her at her apartment, paid for the tickets and popcorn. We got the student special deal. I mean, I'm not Richard Branson. I opted not to get my cinema regular, which is nachos and cheese sauce. Better lay off them, as I was sure the shift was on post-film. We went to see *The Last Song* starring Miley Cyrus.

That choice haunts me to this day. I found it to be the most emotional, heartbreaking and saddest film I'd ever seen. My date didn't. She asked me back to her apartment after the film. It's not what you're thinking, though. It was so I could clean up and get myself together. I cried at the end of the film, down the stairs and through the lobby, while we walked back to her place, and into her pillow as she patted me on the back to console me. The bed was soaking – and not in a good way. This film had broken me. I was hoping she'd say, 'Aw it's so cute, I love guys who are emotionally aware.' She didn't say that. She didn't say anything, actually. I left and avoided her for the remainder of my college life, which turned out to be only four weeks anyway.

JB: So Sarah, we've talked about the people to look out for and those to avoid. Now it's time to take a look at you. There probably won't be too many ladies in the ag science class. You're a rose among the thorns, or nettles or whatever ye have growing up there in Mayo.

JS: You can work this to your advantage as I did way back in 2009, when I was the only male studying home economics for the Leaving Cert in Coláiste Phobal Roscrea. A double class back then was basically speed dating, at least that's how I saw it. I've got a D2 grade to prove it too. Home economics was great, the perfect chance to mix with the opposite sex on their home turf. (No, not the kitchen. I know what ye were thinking. I'm not a sexist.) Not only did I get to try my cheesy chat-up lines on the entire class, including the teacher, but seventeen-year-old me reckoned I had a shot. I didn't. I also learned how to cook and knit without having to go to prison. I was clever (or sneaky, depending at what angle you're coming at this from). I managed to befriend the girls in my class, which resulted in never having to do any homework as they let me copy theirs. I also got the inside scoop on who was dating, who was available and who was into me (not too many) by overhearing conversations between them about other guys' mishaps. This gave me the tools I needed to plot a course to a lady's heart. (Wow, writing this makes me seem like an absolute prick.)

JB: How did you avoid slipping into the friend zone?

JS: Lad, I was playing county minor. You keep forgetting this, I've only mentioned it a million times.

JB: So, armed with this perspective, listen to the lads in your course when they talk about the problems they're having with other girls. (They will talk, trust us. Lads always blab.) Now you're in a position of power, you know their likes and dislikes, so you're in pole position.

Learn from this and don't make the same mistakes they did.

If all this fails, you could just join your local MACRA society in your college. For any readers who don't know what MACRA is, it's what farmers use instead of Tinder. It's basically a society used to get farmers married and ensure there're lots of little farmers running around the farmyards of Ireland. We can guarantee you that within one week of joining MACRA, you'll have a date – if not a husband or a sexually transmitted disease, ha ha.

JS: Lastly, be yourself. Relax and it will all take care of itself. There's someone out there for everyone. Aw, I'm getting all emotional now.

The top ten worst chat-up lines of all time

Never, ever, ever use these. They don't work. (Smacks is speaking from experience here.)

1. I like your legs, what time do they open at?

2. Did you fart? Because you blew me away!

3. How do you like your eggs in the morning? I like mine fertilised.

4. I'm not the best-looking lad in the place, but I'm the only one talking to you.

5. I bet you €20 you won't shift me.

6. Boy: Hello. Girl: I've got a boyfriend. Boy: I've got a goldfish. Girl: What? Boy: Oh sorry, I thought we were talking about irrelevant things in our lives. Can I buy you a drink?

7. Are you my small toe? Because I want to bang you off all the furniture.

8. Hey! Is your name Wi-Fi? Because we have a great connection.

9. Do you like cheese? Because I'm an Easy Single.

10. Are you a parking ticket? Because you've got fine written all over you.

JOBS

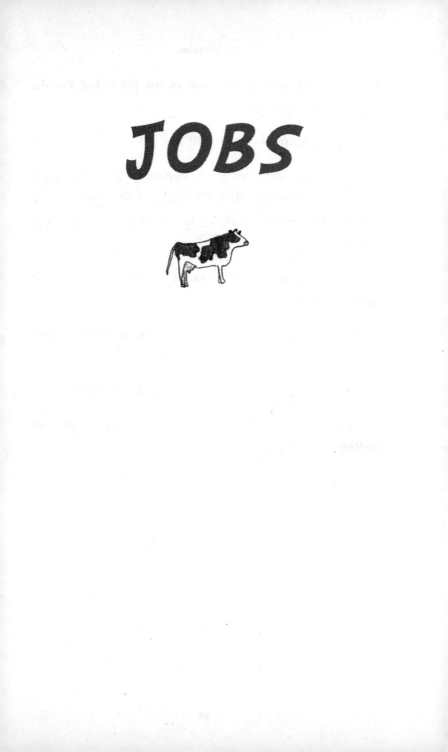

Dear Johnnies,

I've got myself into a sticky situation that I'm hoping ye can help me with.

I absolutely hate my job at the moment (I work in a local supermarket) and to make things worse I shifted this guy who I work with at the Christmas party. The problem is I immediately regretted it, telling my work pals of how awful it was. I genuinely don't fancy the guy. Naturally, word got back to my boss of what happened and what I'd said. To say he wasn't impressed was an understatement, but then again he is a prick. I'm particularly embarrassed because the guy I shifted is the boss's son, and he has a girlfriend.

Neither of them have spoken to me since it happened, which is making it so awkward in work. I've tried making small conversation at coffee breaks to try and break the ice but have had no luck. The problem I have now is I'm looking to take some holidays but I don't know how to approach my boss. Do I acknowledge what happened and what I said? Or do I just pray that he doesn't bring it up? What if he sacks me? I really need this time off and I'm hoping somehow you've got the answers.

Ann-Marie

Dublin

Ann-Marie, don't panic. Most people all around the world hate their jobs and the two of us are no different. We've had all sorts of jobs from fitting tyres to hoovering out spinal cords from pigs. We've done it all and hated every minute of it along the way. One thing to remember is not to make any rash decisions.

←

JS: Like I did. I'm a bit of a nightmare when it comes to jobs. I was class at getting them, it was keeping them which was the problem. When I was working at my local bacon factory, there was one thing that was sacred and that was breakfast. It was the highlight of the day, ripping off the blood-stained uniform and racing down to the canteen for a few greasy sausages. The problem was that on this particular day, I didn't seem to be getting the usual nod from my boss to let me know I could go for breakfast. I asked him what the story was and why wasn't I allowed to go for break when everyone else were already halfway through their breakfast rolls. He replied, 'You'll go when I tell you to go.' His bad form was probably down to the fact myself and his daughter had broken up the day before. So, Ann-Marie, I feel your pain. But I wasn't taking this shit from him. As soon as his back was turned, I was gone. Out to the locker room, changed my clothes and proceeded to walk home. I was done with being treated like dirt. I got home and told my mam, who I knew would support me. How wrong was I. She immediately marched me down the road and back into the factory to apologise to my boss. Not a good look for a nineteen-year-old who thought he was a right Tough Teddy, quitting his job.

JB: Lad, you've had so many jobs the boys down the GAA club were calling you 'Johnny Jobs' for a while. When we lived together, Smacks worked down in Iceland – the frozen-food chain, not the actual country. I remember coming home to the house on my lunch one day to find him in the foetal position on the couch watching *Home and Away*, head to toe in his luminous-orange Iceland uniform. I asked him why he wasn't in work. He told me he'd been let go.

That wasn't exactly the truth. I met a fella who worked in there with Smacks and he informed me Smacks had been having a bit of trouble with his manager. Mainly due to the fact he'd always address him as 'Tony' and insist he was to be clean-shaven, which isn't Smacks's style. (He was modelling himself on Heath Braxton from *Home and Away* at the time but when he shaved, he was more Alf Stewart.) It came to a head when the manager called 'Tony' to the office and gave him a lashing, although poor Smacks had shaved the night before. Smacks was then banished to do a stock-take in the freezer. This fella had tears flowing down his face with laughter when he told me what followed next.

After a while the manager went to check up on Smacks but couldn't find him, so asked the fella, 'Have you seen Tony?' to which he replied, 'I seen him at the front door.' He watched on as the manager walked out the shop entrance to be greeted by the sight of Smacks tearing across the carpark in his red Golf, shouting, 'See ya later, "Tony"!' He was never to reappear there again. Anything to say for yourself, Smacks?

JS: He was a prick.

JB: Ann-Marie, a job is a job at the end of the day and it's handy to fund a few nights out, so don't be hasty and throw in the towel just yet. Your boss won't sack you for something as minor as this. We both worked with a woman who'd been found asleep on the job at least twenty times. One day she was asleep for four hours while baking buns. The buns were fairly well cooked by the time she woke up.

Your issues seemed to have raised their ugly head at the annual Christmas party. A night where madness is allowed and a flirt with your colleagues is as traditional as fighting with your family at Christmas. What's done is done and we don't see a shift at the Christmas party as a bad thing. We've all done it.

JB: Some more than others.

JS: Easy now.

The key here is that you learn from your so-called mistakes. When it comes to next year's Christmas party, please follow these simple instructions to ensure lightning doesn't strike twice.

DOS AND DON'TS AT YOUR CHRISTMAS PARTY

Do: Make an effort

It's important to make an effort at the Christmas party, so dress to impress. It might be the perfect opportunity to meet Mr Right, or at least Mr Right-Now.

JS: During my time in SuperValu, I loved the Christmas parties. A chance to see what everybody looked like out of the uniform. One year we went for a meal and I walked in straight past a table full with the girls who worked in the deli. I wasn't being ignorant, I just didn't recognise them without the hair nets, white jackets and aprons.

Always try to attend. It's a team-bonding night so try to get to know everyone at work, even that weird guy who eats his own snots at lunchtime. He's a person too.

Do: Bust a move

Linking arms at the end of the night and singing at the top of your lungs to 'Fairytale of New York' is a must at every Christmas party. Always take some of the older members of staff out for an auld jive. This shows you're a bit of fun and the life and soul of the party. It's also handy because the older crew have a lot of power in the workplace. So, when you finally bring yourself to ask for that raise, Bridie in accounts will remember fondly the quickstep you shared with her to Joe Dolan's 'Good Looking Woman' and you're on the road to Moneyville.

JB: But don't be too rowdy.

JS: Man, how was I to know that Helen from checkouts had a dodgy hip?

Do: Get your money's worth

In some places we've worked you were given a choice. The Christmas bonus or the Christmas party. We always picked the party. But you can get your revenge for the lack of a bonus. It's quite simple – order the most expensive items on the menu. It's like a protest feast.

JS: I ordered liver pâté at one party. I don't like liver and I also don't like pâté, but it was expensive. Point made.

The staff in these restaurants must find it easy to take orders. If there's fifty people sitting for a meal we promise you all fifty will be having fillet steak. Even if they're vegans. A couple of years of this and you won't be long getting your hands on the bonus.

Do: Buy your boss a drink

Although you probably give out about him every day, he's still your boss. No better time to show that there's no hard feelings by buying him a festive drink. It'll come in handy when he sees you puking your guts up in the jacks on Monday morning because you went for the cure on the Sunday.

JB: Be tactical too. When buying him a drink, get him a shot too and make sure he necks it. That way, when he's dancing on a table at 3 a.m. with a tie around his head, rocking out to AC/DC, you won't be the drunkest person in the room.

Don't: Think this is *Love Actually*

Christmas can give you a false sense of fairy tale. The Christmas party only adds to this. Everyone thinks tonight's the night I'm finally gonna declare my undying love for Peter the stock controller. Please refrain. The problem is, you're not Martine McCutcheon and this is not *Love Actually*. Most romantic Christmas films have happy endings, whereas attempting to lob the gob on poor Peter when you're full to the neck on free wine is not gonna have such a happy ending. We all know how it pans out. You throw the head at Peter. He knocks you back and you end up in the smoking area bawling your eyes out getting consoled by all the girls, all the while claiming you didn't even fancy him anyway. Man, we miss those parties.

Don't: Hog the mic

Karaoke always seems to be the activity of choice for Yuletide parties. We can't understand why. It's great for those who are able to hold a tune, but when John the bookkeeper gives you his rendition of 'Crystal Chandelier' for a third year running, it can get a bit draining. The key to karaoke is to sing while you're still sober. The drunker you get, the more you think you're Beyoncé – when, realistically, you sound more like Beyoncé's dog.

You don't wanna end up like our buddy Nine Inch Niall (we'll let you decipher the nickname). Anyway, Niall was asked to sing a song early in the night but declined, stating, 'I'll have a few pints first.' Fast-forward a few hours and he's got his sixty-five-year-old boss in a headlock as he belts out the Kaiser Chiefs' classic 'I Predict a Riot'. As onlookers, we sort of knew Niall wouldn't be flavour of the week that following Monday.

Don't: Shift in public

The old saying 'Don't shit on your own doorstep' has never been so apt here. If you're going to have a festive fumble with a colleague then at least do it out of sight of your nosy workmates, who are only hoping for a bit of gossip to brighten up their boring lives. Again, our buddy Niall is guilty here. He's normally quite the shy type, but he's also a bit like an owl, he comes alive in the night-time. At this particular party he managed to get the shift for himself.

JS: The problem was it was in front of the entire workforce, managers included, and with a girl from the office who was as shy as he was. It was like a David Attenborough documentary in our local, everyone looking in amazement at this male beast in action, the commentary being provided by yours truly and our fresh-food manager Finbar. He ensured me Monday was gonna be good fun considering they both left the pub together, hand in hand. And true to his word, Finbar was on fire with the slagging right from the off. In the spirit of workplace banter, he tortured Niall and Emma. (Note: this is not her name, it's Sarah. Probably shouldn't say that.) Each hour he would get on the intercom and say, 'Niall and Sarah to the office, please' and then howl laughing through the speakers.

Here at *The 2 Johnnies*, we know you can't mix business and pleasure, which is why we introduced a strict 'Don't screw the crew' motto. It works a treat.

We think the best way to deal with this situation is to just front it out. Knock on your manager's door Monday morning, tell him you need some time off, as simple as that. If he mentions anything about you wearing the face off his son at the Christmas party, just tell him his son was the kissing equivalent of a washing machine. That'll stop him in his tracks. If he's reluctant to give you some time off, fear not, we've got a plan.

Getting time off will be as easy as beating Offaly in a senior hurling match for you now, Ann-Marie, because we're experts when it comes to scamming a few days of work. We've used all sorts of excuses to get some time off over the years. Most of them to pursue being a full-time Johnny, others just to binge on Pringles and nurse a hangover.

SIX EXCUSES TO FOOL YOUR BOSS

1. The 'women trouble' excuse

If there's a phrase that'll guarantee a day off and have managers running to hide in their office, it's 'women trouble'. Men can't deal with it. This can be used not only for a day off but also if you've done anything wrong.

JS: I used work with a girl from my SuperValu days who could play this card so well. She could also cry on demand. She should have been a Hollywood actress by right. She once managed to get a week off because her boyfriend broke it off with her. That's a skill. One day she had tickets to see P!nk perform in Cork and needed to finish early. While our boss was deciding what he wanted on his salad roll, she broke down right on cue. She muttered the famous words when he asked her what was wrong. 'I've got women trouble.' He immediately clammed up and began to turn a similar shade to the beetroot he'd just asked for and immediately agreed to give her the rest of the day off. Genius.

2. The 'dead relative' excuse

This is a tough one to use because you'll eventually run out of relatives. Our buddy down the GAA club has missed training so many times due to the death of his grandparents that it's led us to investigate how many sets of parents this lad actually had. There seems to be a funeral at least once a month. Some people believe it's morally wrong to use such an excuse. They've got a point.

JS: On the other hand, those same people have never been on their hands and knees for ten hours, armed with only soapy water and a toothbrush, attempting to clean underneath a smelly butcher's counter that hasn't been washed since Italia '90. I'm glad I got that off my chest.

3. The 'diarrhoea' excuse

This can be a nasty one to use but is effective nonetheless. It's also one of those ones when you pray karma won't come back and bite you in the arse. Literally.

JS: It's common sense to know that if diagnosed with diarrhoea you cannot work anywhere near food. Having googled this as a sixteen-year-old, I had a lightbulb moment. I was working part-time on a butcher's counter and knew that having 'the runs' would ensure me a day off so I could watch the Super Sunday match, which involved my beloved Liverpool. I called up the boss and explained my illness. I was sure his reply would be 'Okay, I can't have you anywhere near the counter.' Was that his reply? Was it fuck. He proceeded to ask me four more times could I not still come in. I explained it was coming out of me faster than Seamie Callanan onto a loose ball. He eventually gave up. Needless to say, my mother didn't buy the Sunday roast in there anymore.

4. The 'flu' excuse

Ah, the old reliable. You're as sure to get the flu as you are to shift your boss's son at the Christmas party. Sorry Ann-Marie, is it still too soon?

JB: Some people think ah, I'll just tell the boss I have flu and he'll understand. That might work for one day off. But you need to convince him you've got an awful dose. This starts the day before. You need the get the rumour out that the flu is going around. 'Sure isn't poor auld Maureen down the road smothered with the flu? Oh it's rampant.' Once you put this thought into people's heads, it won't come as a shock when you miraculously contract it. Fail to prepare, prepare to fail.

5. The 'annoy him enough' excuse

What most bosses want is a handy life. They don't want staff stressing them out and adding to their already hectic work life. So, if you constantly badger your boss enough for a day off, he'll eventually give in, just to get you away from him. It's essentially killing him with information. And pointless information at that. Normally, something like this should do the trick:

'Oh I've to bring my mother to the hospital blah blah blah ...'

'And then the dog died blah blah blah ...'

'And would you believe I always use Daz with my washing ...'

Trust us here, Ann-Marie. Your boss is a man, we're also men. He hasn't the slightest interest in what you have to say. He just wants to get away from you. If you can keep him shell-shocked for at least two minutes, he'll say yes to anything, least of all time off to make this stop. Our tip here is to ask him for a pay rise while you're at it.

6. The 'just don't turn up' excuse

You could just not turn up and insist that your boss said you can have the day off. Essentially, it's your word against his. The problem with this is it'll only work once.

JB: I've done the whole not-turn-up thing. I executed it better. I was working in our local supermarket for the summer but couldn't get time off to play a hurling match. Not to be put off by this little problem, I showed up for work at ten o'clock as usual. I disappeared at twelve and went off to Clonmel on the bus, played the match and scored a goal and two points. The fun didn't stop there. I also managed to get a liquid lunch in when I arrived back to Cahir. I was back in work for four o'clock and was expecting to be sacked. It was the opposite. No one had even noticed I'd left. I'm obviously that good a worker.

Ann-Marie, you're now armed with the tools to solve this conundrum. Be bold, be brave and just be yourself. As The Killers say, 'it was only a kiss, it was only a kiss'. Although what the fuck would they know? They might have played the 3Arena but they've obviously never been on an office Christmas party with you. Remember, if your boss doesn't give you the time off, try shifting him next year. That's one way to cement a day off.

Dear Johnnies,

How's she cutting? I'm in bad need of some advice. I'm a 23-year-old man from the one and only Co. Carlow. Don't be slagging now, lads. I'm not long graduated from college and have been on the hunt for a job ever since. Just last week I got offered a job by a big financial institution, which I was over the moon with. The problem is the job is based in their Dublin office. I love Carlow, and love living at home. I play GAA with my local club and love going for a few pints with the boys in my local pub. I've been agonising over the decision since the job offer has been on the table. I'm a single man so I don't have any baggage tying me down here. I guess what I need your help with is the big question, in the words of The Clash, 'Should I stay or should I go?'

Don't hold the fact I'm from Carlow against me.

Sound out lads.

Martin

Co. Carlow

JB: Ah lad, get out of Carlow, will ya? If you spend any longer there you'll turn into Richie Kavanagh and before you know it the only hobby you'll have is racing pigeons, and no one wants that.

JS: It's a big move to make so you've got to weigh up the pros and cons. We think the move to the Big Smoke might be a good thing for you but we're biased when it comes to getting the fuck out of Carlow.

BENEFITS OF GOING

Martin, aren't you tired of seeing the same faces fighting each other outside the Foundry? We're joking – we love Carlow really. You're a young man with a lot to offer, and sometimes it's good to get out of the comfort zone and broaden your horizons. For instance, I bet you didn't know there's a train that runs along the street in Dublin. It's called the Luas. It's actually a tourist attraction for most of us country folk.

This move to Dublin could be a fresh start for you. You can be whoever you want in Dublin. We recently met a guy we knew from school and he's living in the Big Smoke. We met him on Grafton Street begging for money. We assumed he'd had a run of bad luck and was homeless. He assured us he was a freegan and that he was living off the land and it was his choice. I know, what's gone wrong with modern Ireland? Now that's not what we recommend for you, Martin, but each to their own. I bet ye don't have freegans in Carlow, eating out of bins. I think they're called locals down your way.

Living in the capital will also help your job prospects. I hate to break it to you, but Google or Facebook won't be setting up their European headquarters in Carlow anytime soon. The dial-up internet would be much too slow.

The Big Smoke will also enhance your chances of meeting a lovely lady to bring home to Mammy. I'm sure Carlow is like most rural towns where there are only a few suitable girls around but they're already shacked up with the local GAA star or a wealthy farmer with loads of road frontage. The story of our lives. That'll all change with your dancing to a Five Megamix in Coppers.

The penultimate reason is that the boom is back in Dublin. There's always something to do to pass the time. Go and visit your cousins in the zoo. Head to the 3Arena and see a hero like Elton John. That beats the social dancing down the parish hall every Sunday evening. I'd rather be at a trendy gig in Dublin than drinking flat 7 Up with a bunch of pensioners as Mike Denver murders another Garth Brooks song.

Lastly and probably the main reason to move – bigger

Penneys. If you're like us and many of our culchie compatriots, there's nothing we love more than a browse around Penneys. And in Dublin the Penneys are on steroids. You'll never want for cheap boxer shorts again.

BENEFITS OF STAYING

The local GAA club is the main reason for lads and ladies not leaving for pastures new. These are the friends you've grown up with and soldiered with all your life. They can be hard to leave behind. Martin, if you're in the same boat as us and are still dreaming of winning silverware for the club and being a local hero, we understand. That's why we haven't left Tipperary. But you don't wanna be one of those auld hurlers on the ditch, crying into your pint of Guinness and insisting you could have been county.

A big factor in staying has to be Mammy's dinners. The plate piled high like the Wicklow Mountains with mashed spuds. It's not only Mammy's dinners that keep us all at home. It's also the constant ironing and washing clothes. The fact that her little darling son can do no wrong in her eyes also helps keep us lads tethered to the apron strings.

Rent in rural Ireland is certainly cheaper. Especially if you're still living at home with the parents afraid to bring a girl home in case your mam gives her the third degree and gets the fine china and the milk jug out. Paying €1000 to live in a wardrobe in Malahide doesn't make the best financial sense.

Another reason we've stayed put in Tipperary is traffic. We can get to our office from our houses in three minutes flat. The same distance in Dublin would take at least six hours. We cry each time we pass the Naas roadworks due to the congestion and that's before we hit the city centre at rush hour. Total gridlock (said in a Jamaican accent like the Malibu ad).

The close-knit communities us culchie folk are used to can be hard to leave behind. It's something as simple as a smile and a wave, even though inevitably we cut the back off them as soon as they're out of sight. We love the feeling of being part of the community, even if that means your nosy neighbours can broadcast what colour knickers your mother has hanging on the line. That's just part of rural life.

Working locally on a farm or building site can be fairly depressing at the best of times but think about the positives. Your boss is sound out and probably manages your Junior B team. So, when ye win a county final and you need a few days off to celebrate, he'll oblige you. Some high-flyer in Ernst & Young or Google won't even know what Junior B is.

The one thing you don't want to happen if you make the big move is that after two months you start wearing a scarf and speaking like you've been born and raised in Portobello. If you feel like you're showing symptoms of the following, come home quick for reality check.

TEN TELL-TALE SIGNS YOU'VE BECOME A CITY SLICKER

1. You eat burritos instead of chicken rolls

The chicken roll is a daily requirement for any true countryman diet. The burrito is the Dublin equivalent but I've never seen a man draw silage for twenty hours straight after eating a burrito. Fact.

2. You're a vegan

I'm telling ya here and now, there isn't a vegan in Carlow, it's against the law. Kale is something you cut down with a strimmer down the country but it's big business in the capital. Being vegan is the new cool thing in Dublin. Don't succumb to this, Martin, your mother will disown you. Imagine telling her you won't eat her Sunday roast. There'll be hell to pay.

3. You don't wear socks

The #anklesout movement is something we're both guilty of from time to time. We strictly only do it when we're in Dublin though. Do not head down your local back home with the ankles out – people in Carlow have only just stopped wearing Doc Martens.

4. You constantly wear earphones

Does nobody talk to each other in Dublin? Whether it's on the Luas, cycling, walking or working, everyone's got a set of earphones in. We're meant to be a country based on having the gift of the gab and the craic. We're starting to think we should replace our emblem of the harp with a set of earphones.

5. You have a funky moustache

Freddie Mercury may have passed on but the moustache is alive and well in hipster Dublin. Moustaches are rarely seen around the country. Normally this look is reserved for old-school Junior B full backs or your grandfather, who possibly may have been involved in some sort of revolution. Sporting a funky handlebar moustache is a sure sign that you're now a fully-fledged city slicker.

6. You hug people when you meet them

We find it really awkward that whenever we're introduced to new people from Dublin they immediately want to throw their arms over us even if our last time meeting them was forty-eight hours ago. We strictly only hug our mammies. We prefer to lead with a firm handshake and eye contact. Proper order.

7. You pronounce your 'ths' instead of your usual 'ds'

We physically cannot pronounce our 'ths' even though we've been asked to during most radio or TV shows we've been on. We'll always pronounce 'mothers' as 'modders'. Martin, don't succumb to this pressure. Keep your accent. Actually come to think of it, the Carlow accent is cat. Maybe consider losing it.

8. You say 'hi' instead of 'welll'

'Welll' is the nation's favourite way to greet somebody. At least it is in Tipperary. 'Hi' is a term we've adopted from our friends over in America. We went to a McDonald's in California last year. The cashier greeted us by saying, 'Hi sir, how are you?' We replied with our usual 'welll'. She stared blankly. We left. I urge anyone reading this book, you included, Martin, to keep 'wellll' alive and kicking in Ireland.

9. You have avocado for breakfast

Anyone telling ya avocados are good for you and an ideal part of a balanced breakfast have obviously never had a breakfast roll from a filling station on a depressing Monday morning. That's a balanced breakfast, it balances perfectly between my two hands. Imagine giving 1991 All-Star hurler of the year Pat Fox an avocado before a Munster final – you'd wake up dead.

10. You believe you're a food critic

Every cool dude who moves to Dublin seems to fancy themselves as a bit of a food expert. Hah – a few months before they were eating a garlic cheese chips off the ground outside their local kebab shop at 3 a.m. Now they're Gordon fucking Ramsey. We were in Dublin recently and asked a friend of ours who's been living in Dublin for a year to recommend somewhere to eat. We ended up eating some sort of rabbit food served up to us by a fella wearing a top hat. Safe to say we won't be asking him again.

THE 2 JOHNNIES' DUBLIN PUB BIBLE

Martin, you mentioned you were a young single man. Now, if like us, you like to do some exploring and see what Dublin has to offer (the nightlife particularly) then we've got you covered. The first time we went out in Dublin we asked for cans of cider, to which the barman replied, 'Do you want a sod of turf with that?' We now know cans of cider are not sold in the capital, so we broadened our knowledge. We can't navigate ourselves from Heuston Station to the Spire but we can tell you every decent pub in Dublin worth visiting.

Ryan's of Camden Street

The Tipperary embassy in Dublin. If you want to talk silage with an ag science student from Monaghan or maybe have your temperature checked by a student nurse from Wexford, Ryan's is your one-stop shop. We love it because they're constantly showing GAA matches on the big screen. We can pop in on a Tuesday night and watch the 2001 All-Ireland hurling final. Last Christmas we played a sold-out show in Whelan's and the following night we were singing

'Flying Without Wings' and crowd-surfing in Ryan's. Both as pleasing as each other. Martin, make this your local.

The Boar's Head

If GAA is your thing you have to pop into the Boar's Head in Dublin city centre. The owner, Hugh, who's a Cavan man, is a hero and has seen everyone from Alex 'Hurricane' Higgins to Páidi Ó Sé pass through the doors (who had a routine of ordering three-quarter full pints of Guinness – these are the kind of great stories you'll hear in there). It's steeped in tradition and is the first stop for the All-Ireland winners, the morning after their triumph. We met a young American man on our travels called John Greene who served in the US army but now puts down his time hurling in San Diego. He'd come over for the All-Ireland weekend and wanted to meet his heroes but found himself stranded at the Red Cow. He proceeded to walk all the way to the Boar's Head from there as he'd heard the craic was mighty. That pretty much sums up this place.

Cassidy's

Sunday evenings in Cassidy's are legendary. Everybody is normally buzzing from a jam-packed day of watching or playing sport or maybe they just don't wanna believe they're back to work on Monday, but the place is always heaving. It's perfect for you, Martin, cos we reckon 90 per cent of the punters are culchies too. One night while we were belting out 'The Black Velvet Band' we noticed the voice coming from the microphone wasn't that of the singer from Rake the Ashes, the house band. It sounded so familiar that we put down our drinks and went to investigate. We were right, we did recognise that voice. It was none other than international rugby referee Nigel Owens, pint in hand, his head turning a shade of red from hitting the high notes. We asked him did he know 'Back Home in Derry'? He didn't.

Temple Bar

Going to Temple Bar is an experience, to say the least. At €8 a pint it's not somewhere we would normally frequent and somewhere we wouldn't advise you to head, Martin, if you want to be able to pay your rent. You won't find too many Irish among the crowds who flock there as we're much too cute for that carry-on. You'll find busloads of Americans, though. They'll be the ones wearing socks and sandals. There's no flies on the yanks though. We once observed a couple order a pint of Guinness and two empty half-pint glasses. When we asked them why, they replied that it was 20 cent dearer to get two half pints as opposed to one full pint. The cheek of them! One Wednesday we were enjoying some music in Temple Bar when we met some ladies from Minnesota, so we decided we'd educate them on Ireland and see how much shite talk they would believe. At one stage we had them fully convinced that in Cork they never had a Thursday. They had a six-day week. Those ladies are probably part of Trump's administration now.

Coppers

'Teachers, students, nurses, guards, I told her I was going to score from 90 yards' – and yes, it works every time. Ah, Coppers. The ultimate culchie hotspot. A place in which everyone insists they won't lose their dignity but invariably always do (and their jackets, we've lost at least ten). It's a magical place where you instantly become a fan of the Spice Girls and the Vengaboys even though you'd never listen to that tripe on a normal day. We'd advise against wearing your best Sunday shoes into Coppers as they'll most likely look like you've spent the day at the Ballinasloe horse fair when you eventually head for a kebab. The fashion on display in Coppers is like nothing I've seen before: you could find a high-flier in his fitted suit, a girl in a ballgown or a fella covered in dust still sporting his Snickers workwear pants after a hard day on site. You won't have to dress trendy to get in – the Carlow look of bootcut jeans, check shirt and brown suede shoes will go down a treat on the dance floor.

Café en Seine

If you want to impress the locals back home or give it the Billy Big Bollocks on Instagram then you have to check out this place. It looks like something from The Great Gatsby. The first night we set foot in there, we came home with cricks in our necks from admiring the views. But don't make the same mistake we did: we thought we were the big men having our Christmas night out. We were a few pints in when we got a brainwave to head to Café en Seine – nothing else would do but champagne for the boys! It was all well and good till we checked the online banking the following morning. We haven't been back since.

O'Donoghue's

JS: This traditional pub makes it onto the list as it's where Johnny B's parents first went on a date. JB, I'll leave this one to you.

JB: Not a hundred yards from Stephen's Green is one of the finest bars in the capital. Opened by Paddy and Maureen O'Donoghue in 1934, it's become synonymous with Irish music and pints of the black stuff. They've even painted the outside black and white, just in case there was any doubt about their position on porter. It wouldn't be known for its cocktails.

O'Donoghue's holds a special place in my heart because it's where my father took my mother on their first date. My dad is proper Tipperary and my mam is a Dub. So after a chance meeting through family friends, where could a Tipp man possibly take a Dublin girl? Croke Park of course, and the 1977 All-Ireland Football Final, Dublin vs Armagh. Father just happened to have two tickets. But where to after? There was no TripAdvisor back then, and my father had only heard of one pub in the whole of Dublin, which was where folk music legends The Dubliners and The Wolfe Tones had their trad sessions, so O'Donoghue's it was. Dublin beat Armagh and Jimmy Keaveney was top scorer that year with 2–27, but my father was the real winner that day. Pulled the best-looking woman in Dublin. I asked him about it recently and he said, 'Joe Kernan was very good for Armagh. He went on to be manager you know – won an All-Ireland too.'

O'Donoghue's, pints, trad and romance.

We recommend you make the move. Nothing ventured nothing gained. If it turns out you hate Dublin you can always just come home. It's not a million miles away and there's no shame in going back.

JB: On the other hand, if you love Dublin then it's happy days, Joe Hayes. Although get back to the dolmen county to raise your family – you don't want to be rearing kids who eat avocados and speak like Brian O'Driscoll.

JS: Also, the rent will cripple ya with a family and that money could be better used by investing it in your kids' fledgling GAA careers – maybe Carlow might actually win something then! All the best.

If anyone reading this book has been affected by this chapter and feels they're not keeping it country enough, fear not. Take this perfectly designed quiz to test your culchie knowledge:

HOW CULCHIE ARE YOU?

1. Who wrote the song 'Hit the Diff'?

2. Who is the lead singer of The Saw Doctors?

3. Who won the 1995 All-Ireland hurling final?

4. The Marquee in Dromlish is located in which county?

5. Which county is Supermac's from?

6. Belgian Blue is a type of what?

7. What colour is a John Deere tractor?

8. What does ICA stand for?

9. During which month are the ploughing championships traditionally held?

10. Bonus question: Where were the 1993 ploughing championships held?

11. Who's the female presenter of *Ear to the Ground*?

12. Who was Miley's father in *Glenroe*?

13. What time is dinner time in a country household?

14. In which county is Lisdoonvarna?

15. From which county is Daniel O'Donnell?

16. What does *Macra na Feirme* mean in English?

17. Complete this classic sandwich: ham and _____ .

18. In the bog, what's known to eat ya?

19. Pat Shortt and Jon Kenny were known as what?

20. What is the Wexford emblem?

*See answers on page 207.

11 or under: if you get fewer than five questions right you're about as culchie as an oat-milk cappuccino. You need to be put in a room and have The Saw Doctors boomed at you until you become a culchie again. Hang your head in shame. You've let down the God of Culchie, Jimmy Buckley.

12 or over: A score of 12 or more means you're as culchie as Miley shifting Fidelma in the hay sheds. You're a culchie genius – now go and reward yourself by strimming a few hedges and giving out about your neighbours.

Dear Johnnies,

How's things in Cahir? All quiet here in Annacarty, west Tipperary. Just looking for yer opinion on moving abroad. Two men like yourselves who have seen a bit of the world. I'm hearing stories about lads earning a fortune in the mines in Australia and beach parties in San Diego, but no way of knowing if they'll live up to the hype. I'm 21, a recently qualified quantity surveyor and while there are bits of work going in Ireland, it's mostly in Cork and Dublin. If I was going to move to Dublin and spend all my wages on rent, I'd nearly be as well off to head abroad and try working out there for a while. I could make an absolute disaster for the thing too and be home to Mammy in a week. I'm not sure where I would move to. Yer thoughts?

Dan

Co. Tipperary

Thanks for your letter, Dan.

In 1992 Clint Eastwood made a cowboy film called *Unforgiven* about an old hitman taking one last job. There's knife fights, cattle rustling, fellas getting shot over card games, all set in the untamed wilderness of America's Wild West, in the dusty, one-horse crossroads of a village named Big Whiskey. Well, Dan, Big Whiskey is how the rest of Tipp views Annacarty. Apart from the reasonably competitive senior hurling club and the community-run shop, it's the Wild West for sure.

JB: We went into the shop one day after attending a funeral in the village. I said, 'Hello.' She said, 'You're not from the parish.' She was spot on. I'm not.

Small towns and villages can be a great place to live, depending on what you're after. We're getting the feeling that you've caught the bug, Dan. Not what you were up to out the back of Jerry Jack's pub, but the travel bug. Us Irish are known for it – the travelling, I mean. In the sixth century, a priest from Tralee named Brendan is said to have sailed to America on a boat made of timber and leather – 900 years before Christopher Columbus. The Kerry man didn't colonise the continent, though. He just went for an auld look around and came home to Kerry. Yup – the kingdom. He might not have ever made it to America but we like to claim him, like the big Offaly head on Barack Obama. It's estimated that as many as 4.5 million Irish arrived in America between 1820 and 1930. Now I just got that off Google, but the point is, the Irish are no strangers to travel.

If you're going to move abroad for a while, here are some of the places we recommend:

THE UAE

What is it? The United Arab Emirates, the country that has Dubai and Abu Dhabi.

Where is it? The Middle East, to the right of Saudi Arabia and below Iran.

Why go there? Big money.

Get your head around this, Dan, there's no taxman here. They have so much money from oil, the government don't need to tax anyone. The stuff is coming up out of the ground. They actually give money to their citizens, who are known as Emirati. I know what you're thinking: marry one of them and live the good life. Not going to happen, no matter how many years you played county minor. You'd have a better chance of Annacarty winning the World

Cup than one of the locals letting their daughter marry a European. They wouldn't be great for mixing and having the craic. They like to keep to themselves and have their own craic. So, you could work there and not really know any locals. It's not like they'll be stacking shelves in Spar. They get sent money in the post by the government. They're all rolling in it. It's important to consider the big culture change if moving here. When the religious festival of Ramadan comes around, they don't eat or drink during the day, and lad it does be roasting out there, fair play to them. You just have to eat in a private section of the restaurant designated for foreigners. They don't drink, but by God the Irish out there make up for them.

The weather

It's absolutely roasting out there, Dan. Fifty degrees some days. You'll need a lot of sunscreen. You could fry a sausage on your shovel, except if you're coming this far, it won't be to dig holes and lay blocks.

Pool parties

If you have Instagram, then you've seen young wans in bikinis posing for photos with their arse cheeks pressed up against the glass wall of a fancy swimming pool, or in a fancy club that does fancy cocktails, and aren't they all having the time of their life out in Dubai. They might be, but it's costing the price of a small farm every time you buy a round. God love the auld Middle East bar staff – maybe it's because none of them drink themselves that they aren't able to keep it pucked out to the Paddies. Many of your nights out in the UAE will be with other Irish, in Irish-friendly bars. Not like Durty Nellie's in Santa Ponsa, a little swankier than that (most of the time) and it'll be a 'drunch' brunch, where you get scuttered – a flat fee and it's all you can drink. That's not a typo. So please pace yourself. We heard of an Irish couple who met in a bar and were shifting the face off each other in the back of a taxi. The taxi man didn't appreciate their lack of modesty and dropped them off at the police station where they were arrested. Although in the compounds and private bars it's great craic and gets fairly wild, it is still a Muslim country and you have to respect their way of life.

Work

There's plenty of it. The vast majority of Irish in the UAE are teachers. I know you're from Annacarty but your English is still good enough. Teachers are well paid and accommodation is thrown in too. Nice gaffs out there, Dan, proper apartments, no college housing estates to be seen. Chances of a sing-song and a game of headers and volleys breaking out on the street in the middle of the night? Fairly slim. There's construction work to be got too, and as a QS you should be able to pick up work through an agency at first (you'll need the experience) and then go hunting for the big job after a while.

Pros: You'll get a tan and earn good money.

Cons: You'll get sunburnt and spend all your money.

Suited to: Teachers who like to party.

THE USA

What is it? Rappers, supermodels and big lads eating burgers.

Where is it? West of Kerry.

Why go there? It's the land of opportunity.

'Have a nice day!' That's the kind of tripe you'll get in the States. Why? It's the culture. All trying to impress, to climb the ladder. They invented the American dream – work hard and you can achieve anything. Forty million Americans still live in poverty, but Dan, you have what all forty million of them lack – neck. Pure Irish neck. The bit of chat, a wink and a nod, the gift of the gab and absolutely zero inhibitions. It's 3,113 miles from New York to Mammy's house in Annacarty, and she can't see what you're at.

The weather

New York in summer: a sweat box, air conditioning on everywhere. New York in winter could be under four feet of snow. The West Coast cities like San Fran and San Diego are much more chilled.

Work

Irish people generally do quite well in America. Apart from the aforementioned Irish sweet talk, we're hard workers when we go away. In that sense it can be the land of opportunity. Any Irish lad we've met or heard from out there is either working in construction or bartending. And boy do they put in a good shift. Bartending in America is actually a potentially lucrative career path. Much more than pulling pints in Tipp. Speaking of Tipp, it's because of tipping that barmen, and especially Irish barmen, do so well. Learn the auld craic, learn the sports teams, the local area and have the chats with all your clientele. The Americans appreciate good, prompt service and they're prepared to pay or tip for it. Have you ever been in a restaurant in Ireland and you're not completely satisfied with your meal, but then the lovely waitress comes around and asks 'Is everything OK folks?' And we can't say 'Yes, fantastic' quick enough. Well, that don't happen in America. If they're not happy, you better believe you'll hear about it.

In the construction sector, it's mostly Irish and South Americans doing the dirty work, so having a cúpla focal of Spanish would do no harm. You as a QS should have no bother picking up employment. And plenty of lads trained as 'Aer Lingus carpenters': read a book on the flight over; talked the rest of their way into the job.

Things to do

The East Coast: to work hard, play hard. The West Coast: to chill out – they surf, they eat burritos, they like good coffee. California legalised weed and there's a fair bang of it around San Fran. You'd be as well to stay away from that stuff. As an immigrant you need to be on your best behaviour or they'll have you on a plane back to Mammy faster than you can say 'My uncle's a guard.' There's so much to see and do in America: busy night life, lakes, mountains, festivals. Go to Coachella and get a photo in front of the big Ferris wheel. All the boys at home will think you've turned into a complete melt.

Mind yourself

America is nice if you stay in the nice areas. Rent in the major cities like LA can be extortionate but don't think, 'Compton, ah ya I've heard of that, I'll head down there.' Dan, watch the movie *Boyz n the Hood* before you go. This may not be 100 per cent accurate, but as far as we know, everyone in America has a gun. They also might be part of a gang, so learn their secret handshake and be careful what you say about 2Pac.

Some lads marry an American just to get the visa. Might sound like a plan until she turns up with the divorce papers, looking for half the farm in Annacarty.

Find the Irish

Could apply to every country, but in America more than anywhere else, the Irish have created their own vibrant community within the community. If you need a job, join the GAA team – wherever you are in the States, there'll be a GAA team. If you want to work Monday, you better play well Sunday. Even if you aren't All-Star quality, you'll be better than the American lads who play. They often don't understand the rules, but they'll chop you in two with a hurley all the same.

Pros: Lots to see, money to be made, great standard of living.

Cons: You may pick up a horrendous accent. You'll probably put on three stone in weight from all the food. Most fast food places are durt, yet taste so good. Also, you may be deported as it can be hard to get a work visa.

Suited to: Smooth-talking, hardworking young Marty Whelan types.

AUSTRALIA

What is it? A continent, apparently.

Where is it? Below China.

Why go there? Meet the young wans off *Home and Away*.

'Throw another shrimp on the barbie'; 'g'day mate'; 'a dingo took my baby'. Just some of the cultural highlights Australia has given the world. When we were young, we saw the film *Crocodile Dundee*, about an Aussie guy who could tame wild bulls, survive in the wild and disappear into the wind. The only thing accurate about that film was the lads in sleeveless vests and mullets, sitting around drinking small tins of beer. They're real. Australians in general are good craic and you should be able to make many friends with the locals. They speak English, which is handy. Although being from Tipp, you may have to repeat yourself a bit.

JB: I had elderly Australian relatives over once. I'd say, 'Well, how's it going?' and they'd just stare back at me like I was speaking Swahili. I thought one of them was deaf for the first few days. I was at home learning sign language, turns out I just talk like a caveman.

The craic

No doubt about it, Australia is great craic. It's full of Irish too, like a giant Tramore, or Salthill, but without the shaky amusements and radioactive candy floss. It's a real outdoorsy country and the Aussies love to be outside in the sun, drinking a few bottles of beer and we mean a few – the Irish obviously take it to the next level and as our next-door neighbour used to say, 'There's only so many times I can listen to the "The Fields of Athenry".' The locals, like us, are also big into activities – they are a sports-mad nation. The cities especially have become cosmopolitan and everyone is keeping fit and eating salad and all that carry-on. A friend of ours from home, who is a fairly chunky lad, once told us, 'Some dose – at home people think I'm a rugby player, out here I'm just a fat fuck.'

You can have swanky rooftop bars in Sydney, where you'll enjoy a $30 cocktail, very nice. You could also do it the way many Irish do it, spend your weekends between Brisbane's two Irish bars. In one of them is a man playing guitar and singing a few rebel songs, you know yourself. But this lad gets so into it that he keeps breaking the skin on any bodhran they give him, so now he has a microphone in a plastic watering can, and he just bates that with a stick. Beat that, Snoop Dogg. Mighty craic to be had, but also easy to slip into going out every weekend and spending all your hard-earned Aussie dollars.

Some money in the mines

A lad we know left town without the price of a trowel and came home at Christmas wearing a gold watch, casually telling the entire pub he paid $2,500 for it in Dubai on the way back. I think the entire pub would have preferred he bought us all a round and just checked the time on his phone!

We heard stories of guys earning two or three grand a week down the mines, driving machines, digging, whatever they do down a mine. We've never worked down a mine, Dan, so it could be like the seven dwarfs with pickaxes for all we know. Mostly constructing new mines for zinc and that stuff they put in phone batteries. The thing about mines is, they're fair far away. You can't have a mine out the back of the pub. You won't be home to watch Judge Judy on your lunch break. It's often a three-week swing, twenty-one days straight working, then home for a week. You'll earn good money and there'll be nowhere to spend it either, cos you'll be living beside the mine. Remember in school when ye had a Portakabin that was used as a classroom for all the mad, crayon-eating young fellas? Well that's what your accommodation will be like. It'll be plenty warm. You'll have a gym and TV, but no sessions. Most mines breathalyse the staff each morning. No amount of chewing gum and 'Ah I have a bit of a cold, boss' will work here.

Be careful not to go completely buck wild when you get back to the city for your week off. You'll probably have to rent a room in a house even though you're only there one week in four. It's a tough-enough life. Most lads only do a year or two full-time in the mines before it drives them mad. There's work in town, too: construction, teaching, they also love Irish nurses, (don't we all, says Johnny Smacks). Big money to be earned but easy to spend it too.

Because of the extreme heat, the Australians start and finish early. By one o'clock Friday, with any luck, you'll have a scooner of beer in your hand. (A scooner is a 425ml glass. They reckon your beer would be gone warm by the time you reached the end of a pint. They've never been to Annacarty.)

Things to watch out for

They have snakes. Not the kind your ex-girlfriend posts about on Facebook, but actual snakes. Spiders that can eat a man's head, too. We may have made that up. Other than that, and the crocodiles, the outdoors are great Down Under. Beautiful beaches. Spoiler alert, they have sharks too. Actually, ya know what? Just stay in Tipperary. It's be safer.

Things to see

Uluru, formerly known as Ayers Rock. It's the third most visited attraction in the country, and you guessed it, it's a rock. Formed 550 million years ago and sacred to the indigenous Australians.

JS: Isn't there a quarry near Annacarty if he wanted to see rock?

The Great Barrier Reef. Now this is something you won't get in Tipperary. The world's largest coral reef system. You can snorkel or scuba dive around it. Swim with strange-looking fish and German tourists. The vivid colours and bright collection of 900 islands can be seen from space. No need to go all the way out there to see it so.

Sydney Opera House. The most-visited attraction in

Australia. You know the one we're talking about, the building that looks like someone spilled a giant tin of Pringles. It's cool to look at, but how often you'd go to the opera is a different story, Dan. I can see it here on Google Images, and I'm at home in my shorts.

Most people who move to Australia go for work, make money, and come home in three or four years. Others stay on and live there. With your qualification, you'd get your residency handy enough as long as you don't wreck the place and get arrested, which is easy enough to do if you're drunk and falling around central Sydney. You need ID just to get into a bar, no matter your age. They actually scan it in most places, high-tech lads. What you got up to out the back of Jerry Jacks won't fly here.

Pros: Money to be made. Nice people, good weather, the great outdoors.

Cons: Snakes, spiders, sharks, crocodiles. They don't all look like yer wan off Home and Away. Also, kangaroos can punch you in the face.

Suited to: Tradesmen who are willing to work and are able to handle themselves in a kangaroo fight.

DENMARK

JS: You're having a top laugh now, lad.

JB: It has very few snakes and spiders.

The capital city Copenhagen is very multicultural, with plenty of Irish and British living and working happy out. Outside of Copenhagen, the rest of the country is pure misery, rain, cows and nothing happening, like Offaly. The capital is the only place to go. There's a bridge going from there to the Swedish city of Malmö. You can get the train, look at Malmö, realise it's shit and turn back.

They must have a very active Tidy Towns committee in Copenhagen cos the place is shining. No rubbish, no hassle on the streets. It's a very safe, tidy, modern city. They all cycle bikes.

JS: Bloody hippies, no way I'm going.

Cycling actually works grand because there are loads of safe cycleways, not like cycling in Dublin where you'd be safer on a rodeo bull. All the cycling keeps the air clean and the city centre fairly quiet from the lack of traffic noise. They cycle on a night out, then at the end of a night's partying, they cycle home! They're straightforward, easy-going people. As the Danish saying goes, 'If you don't have a beer or a cigarette in your hand, what are you up to?'

You're allowed to drink on the streets. They do it with a bit of class, not like 'Donegal Tuesday' in Galway University, which is somewhere between Mardi Gras and the Ploughing Championships.

Weather

Like Ireland but slightly less rain. Which is good cos you'll be out in it when you're cycling.

Work

Plenty of tech jobs going. They're crying out for young people. If you get a degree there, they'll actually pay you to stay in the country. You'd want it, it's a pricey enough place to live. You wouldn't be going over there to mix cement.

The people

Straight out of an IKEA advert, or the villains in a James Bond movie. Tall, slim, blond, smoking a fag and drinking coffee. The best-dressed race of people we've ever seen. Hard to believe they're the same crowd who came and beat up the monks all those years ago. That was the eighth century and they were preforming under the name 'Vikings', but we remember. Ye still owe us a few gold crucifixes, lads. Nowadays the Danish are friendly, educated and up for a few pints. They rarely invade anywhere anymore.

Things to see and do

There's an old army barracks near Copenhagen that was abandoned by the military, then in 1971 a bunch of hippy lads started squatting and have been living there ever since. Christiania covers nineteen acres and has about a thousand residents. Proper 1970s hippy job. Deffo worth going to see. They sell weed on the streets there, and it's like everyone's happy out, but the boys selling it are not to be messed with. A serious crowd of hardy bucks, worse than the Tipp Town Massive. Great for a day trip but mind yourself.

Copenhagen itself has an old-school nightclub scene, former abattoirs that have been converted into rave spots. Wilder than Buck's in west Tipperary on Junior Cert results night.

The Danish invented amusement parks and there are a few lovely old ones to visit. They have a bunch of museums, churches, castles, all that craic. It's a nice place to hang out.

Pros: Good standard of living. In the EU, easy to visit home. The Viking Gaels GAA team in Copenhagen have a sexy jersey.

Cons: They don't use the euro. Weather is damp. You have to like cycling.

Suited to: People with degrees in tech or engineering. Hippies and hipsters.

ENGLAND

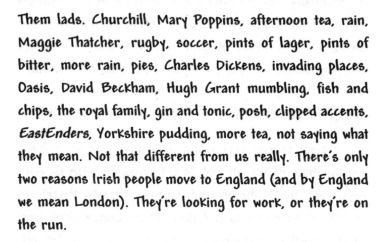

Them lads. Churchill, Mary Poppins, afternoon tea, rain, Maggie Thatcher, rugby, soccer, pints of lager, pints of bitter, more rain, pies, Charles Dickens, invading places, Oasis, David Beckham, Hugh Grant mumbling, fish and chips, the royal family, gin and tonic, posh, clipped accents, *EastEnders*, Yorkshire pudding, more tea, not saying what they mean. Not that different from us really. There's only two reasons Irish people move to England (and by England we mean London). They're looking for work, or they're on the run.

Plenty of work going in England, Dan. The Irish are well in the construction industry since we first went over there in the seventies with a shovel and a donkey jacket. They needed men to dig holes and by God did we dig, nearly dug all the way home. You, as a QS, will be hoping to keep your hands blister-free.

Living standards

Rent in London, like Dublin, is crazy. Your landlord may as well kidnap your child and send you a ransom note. It gets cheaper the farther out you go, but then you have to spend more time on the train. The London Underground works fairly well. But if you're on the Tube, remember they're English and don't talk to each other. Don't take it personally. To strike up a conversation with a stranger could get you locked up. The sweat and smell of pickpockets, along with the stress of your commute, should help you lose any weight you put on. Apart from that, it's not bad.

Things to see and do

It's a great tourist destination, Big Ben, London Bridge, Buckingham Palace, all that jazz. But you're Irish so you'll walk past these things and mutter 'Bloody Brits' cos you're not sure how to feel about them. London has many excellent galleries, museums, theatres, etc. if you're into that. London also gets all the good music gigs. Chances of The Rolling Stones doing a show in Annacarty are slim enough, but every act in the world hits London. So, plenty to go see and do at night-time.

Plenty of Irish

If you wanted to work and socialise only with other Irish

people, then this could easily be done in London. We're everywhere. Fifteen GAA clubs and tonnes of Irish bars should provide enough cover.

Pros: Easy to get to. Book the flight early and it's cheaper than the train to Portarlington. You'll be home for every christening and county final. They speak English.

Cons: It's too close. Mother will be on to ya to come home all the time. They don't use the euro. The English will hit you with a potato joke every day.

Suited to: The 'happy to be away from home' guy, must be fond of work.

JS: That rules me out.

Dear Johnnies,

How are ye, ye pair of mad scones? I'm looking for yer help. Myself and my boyfriend Wayne are planning on going on a sun holiday abroad this summer. We've been together for eight months now and said we'd head away for our one-year anniversary. The problem is I really enjoy being active, whether it's climbing a mountain or sightseeing, I love being constantly on the go and also enjoy some nice meals! Who doesn't like being wined and dined? My boyfriend is the opposite. He's told me all he wants to do is 'lie by the pool and drink a heap of cheap pints' – his words, not mine. He's already talking about how many bottles he could fit into the suitcase from duty-free (he's from Cavan). As long as there's an Irish bar that shows GAA he'll be a happy man. If I had to put up with a week of that crap, I think we'd be flying home on separate flights. Is there any way we can go on a holiday together that we both would enjoy? Or some suggestions on what activities we can do while on holidays? Also, any tips on heading abroad as I've never holidayed outside Ireland before. Salthill in Galway was as far as I've got! I'm open to all suggestions as my fella has left the final decision up to me, as per usual. Hope ye guys can help me out.

Thanks a million,

Emma, a proud Kerry woman

Emma, we're in shock. We can't believe a man from Cavan and a woman from Kerry are willing to part with their money for something as exotic as a foreign holiday. Fair play to ye, you're bucking the trend. What you don't want to do here is go off booking a holiday willy-nilly and end up hating it. That's where we come in. We won't let that happen. We're gonna tell you everything ye need to know like.

JB: What type of holiday you're going on.

JS: Who you're going on holiday with.

JB: When you're going on holiday.

JS: That's if you're going on holiday at all.

First things first, you need to know what type of holiday you're looking for. There's a lot of different types of breaks ye can go on, so choose wisely.

THE TRADITIONAL COUPLES' HOLIDAY

Ah yes, the traditional couples' holiday. Where holding hands, romantic walks and candlelight dinners are wholly acceptable. Those three things never happen at home though. If you attempted to hold hands with your other half while you were out doing the big shop in SuperValu on a Friday they'd jump out the window to avoid such public displays of affections. These holidays provide a good chance to get to spend some quality one-on-one time together, but be careful because this can also have a detrimental effect on the relationship. Some men think, 'Sure it's only the two of us, we'll spend the week in the bedroom.' The sun can do strange things to people. Trying to – in the words of Will Smith – 'get jiggy wit it' can prove difficult, particularly if you've been stingy with the auld factor 50 during the day. Trying to initiative 'relations' with your other half can prove difficult when they're the colour of a beetroot and slathering themselves in yoghurt to ease the pain. (Note: natural yoghurt genuinely stops the sting of sunburn. You're welcome.)

Couples' getaways can get quite boring especially as it's your first holiday together. Here's a genius little tip – make friends with another couple on the first night. That way Wayne has a drinking buddy and someone to go to the Irish bar with on a Sunday to watch all the GAA action. Emma, this gives you a bit of time to do the things you like to do, and most likely a bit of peace and quiet, and a chance to ring your friends at home and complain about Wayne. That's perfectly normal.

Recommended destination: Lanzarote

THE COUPLES' GROUP HOLIDAY

This type of holiday falls somewhere between a couples' holiday and a lads/girls' holiday. It normally involves a group of friends dragging their resentful other halves away. We've been on these holidays before and they can be wild. We once witnessed a couple who were sharing the sofa bed come back after a night out, remove all the shelves from the fridge and proceed to sleep on the floor with their heads in the vegetable drawer. When we asked what they were doing the fella replied, 'We got sunburnt today so we're sleeping in here to keep cool.' Needless to say, they weren't the brightest and we felt that 4 a.m. probably wasn't the best time to lecture them on the hazards of sleeping in a fridge. When they woke the next morning with their throats swollen from the fridge fumes they soon realised these hazards. It was fun, though, watching on as they drank their cocktails in between shots of Difflam.

The main problem on on these trips is a particular bugbear of ours – splitting the bill. 'Let's split the bill,' shouts one genius at the table. And although you and your partner only had a starter Caesar salad each, you're now footing the bill for Big Jim who's scoffed a T-bone the size of a football along with a gallon of red wine.

Still, with Wayne being a Cavan man he won't put up with this anyway, so our advice, Emma, is that this is the perfect holiday for you guys. It's a couples holiday that still allows you time away from each other, which – trust us – you'll need on your first foray together.

Recommended destination: Crete

THE FAMILY HOLIDAY

The perfect way to test your relationship. If he can deal with your parents, your nieces and nephews then surely the man is a keeper. The problem with these types of holidays is the screaming kids. If it's bad being stuck beside a toddler on a Ryanair flight for three hours, imagine spending a week or more with one. Also, you may not want to expose Wayne to the dangers of your crazy and sometimes inappropriate uncle (every family in Ireland has one) just yet.

The only good thing about a family holiday is that there's going to be someone from the party who, through illness of laziness, feels the need to rent a mobility scooter. Make the most of it – nobody likes walking in blazing hot sun. We rent one every time we go abroad. In fact, we rent a double seater, coasting down the strip like Lloyd and Harry from *Dumb and Dumber*. On the whole, though, our advice is to swerve the family holiday. You don't want to scare Wayne away for good.

Recommended destination: Costa del Sol

THE LADS'/GIRLS' HOLIDAY

If €9 for a litre of vodka makes you excited, you like visiting A&E at least once on a holiday and bringing one of your friends home crying each night because they didn't get the shift then a lads/girls' holiday is for you. Nobody said you had to go on a couples' holiday – you could easily travel separately. These types of holidays are known for being pure carnage – the type of holiday where you spend every night in the same Irish bar, linking arms with strangers and belting out 'Dirty Old Town' at the top of your lungs.

JS: On my first night on a lads' holiday I was already a bit fuzzy as the plane came in to land – the stack of mini cans of beer in my lap can attest to that. We went on a pub crawl as soon as we arrived at the resort. This particular crawl resulted in me crawling into the back of an ambulance and into the local A&E where I got five stitches over my left eye. We felt like the Inbetweeners.

It was a nice way to remember the holiday and cheaper than a tattoo as well as being a sure-fire way to remember to drink sensibly. Attempting to slide down three flights of stairs on the bannister is never a good idea, fuzzy or not.

If choosing this holiday, we recommend you take an extra week off work when you return. Trust us, you'll be glad you did.

Recommended destination: Santa Ponsa

THE ADVENTURE HOLIDAY

JS: I want to go on record as saying I don't believe in adventure holidays. Holidays are for relaxing. I mean, walking up the side of a mountain in 40-degree heat is not relaxing, and nor is cycling the length of Spain. Do these people enjoy the discomfort of sitting on a saddle for a week? I'm gonna have to leave this one to Johnny B.

Recommended destination: Bali or Trabolgan in Cork.

BE PREPARED

JB: When jetting off ye have to start with the basics.

Make sure you're well prepared, since travelling can be stressful enough. No offence to Wayne but he sounds like the lad who only goes looking for his passport the night before and then realises it expired eight years ago.

My passport caused big problems on our first trip to America. I'm a bit of a rocker, but I used to be hardcore, long hair and beard. I thought I looked badass. US security clearance thought I looked gone off. Not saying they discriminate, just saying I was always chosen for those random selection tests, the ones where they swab your body and bag for explosives. Big Robinson Crusoe head on me. The passport photo looked like Tom Hanks in *Cast Away*. So, make sure Wayne looks his best in his photo ID and not like a security threat.

SNIFF OUT THE BARGAINS

JS: After spending the few auld few pound on the hollibops, I'm sure Wayne, being a true Cavan man, will want to rein in the spending a little bit. That starts in the airport, before you've even got on the flight. Airports will burn a hole in your pocket faster than a woman in Penneys on payday.

JB: Smacks gets great enjoyment out of me when I travel. Like a newborn baby, all I do is sleep, poo and eat. I try not to cry on the plane. I am not ashamed to say it lads, I bring my own sandwiches on the flight. Yes, just like out of the boot of your car on Munster final day, I bring the home-made ham sandwiches. Tinfoil may set off the scanner, so go with cling film. A lunch box is just too bulky, unless you're bringing home-made cake or tart too, then fair enough. Laugh all you want, but when the air hostess comes around selling you the world's smallest breakfast roll for €9, you'll be glad of the Tipperary packed lunch.

Note: The US pre-clearance guys don't allow certain sandwich fillers on board, for some reason. But I told the cop it was turkey and he let me through. All I need to do now is figure out how to get a kettle into my carry-on bag.

JS: Don't even get me started with the on-flight prices. Airlines are clever, and they know we're Irish, and they know we like a drink, and they know we don't care what the price is because 'Ah sure, we're on holiday.' Irish people are easy to pick out on any flight. They're normally reading their local paper – in our case *The Tipperary Star* – balancing several mini bottles of gin/whiskey on their tray table and somehow managing to munch on a box of salt-and-vinegar Pringles. What is it with Irish people's obsession with Pringles on planes? It's an epidemic. They don't even care a snack-size pot costs seven euro! 'Ah sure, we're on holiday.'

JB: Another tip to save a few euro may be frowned upon by some, but I think it's genius. Never pay for sunbeds at the beach. Yes, there will be some guy trying to sting you for fifteen euros' worth of rental for the day. We're Irish! We don't even like renting houses, never mind sunbeds! Use your Irish charm and insist you paid him already. If he asks for proof, tell him your ticket blew away. Genuinely, this works, but in the off chance it doesn't, try plan B, which is to keep moving from one sunbed to another. It's a game of cat and mouse but you'll always win.

JS: If you're prone to some refreshing alcoholic beverages on your holidays (I have yet to meet an Irish holiday maker who isn't), you need to make the most of happy hour. This essentially is a chance for you to get twice as pissed for half the price. You'll know if a bar has a good happy hour simply by the clientele. If there's a platter of fat, middle-aged English men with bulldog tattoos turning a shade of hot pink outside, odds are there's a cracking happy hour taking place inside.

SPOT THE IRISH

JS: If you find yourself at a loose end while Wayne skulls cheap grog, a great game to play is what I call Spot the Irish. It's quite simple really – you basically people-watch from a safe distance and guess whether the person you've been awkwardly staring at across the pool is Irish or not. They're normally quite easy to identify because they'll either be milk-bottle white or a shade of pink that resembles a freshly grilled rasher. Irish holiday-goers have the monopoly on this particular shade of pink. And if they're ginger and hiding under a gigantic Mary Poppins umbrella? They're definitely Irish.

JB: A Few years ago, I went on a couples' holiday to Lanzarote. While chilling by the pool we started to play a game of Spot the Irish. We picked out one big bruiser of a man who had the head of a Dublin taxi driver and the neck of a guard. He was super tanned, bursting out of his Speedos and he was definitely Irish. We knew this as soon as he asked the barman for 'two San Miguel there bud, when you're ready' in a thick Finglas accent.

His most disgusting feature though, was a huge tattoo across his back. It said *ANN* in block capitals, thick and black. His wife was on the sunlounger next to him, so we assumed she was Ann.

The next day, while perusing the strip and sampling a few local establishments, we came across a Moroccan lad selling those surfer-dude chains and doing temporary tattoos. So, full of half-price Amstel, myself and my girl decided we'd get matching *ANN* tattoos on our backs, exact same as our big buster back at the resort. Hilarious. We went out and had a great night.

Next morning, the fear landed hard. We'd normally start the day with a dip in the pool to freshen up, but there, 20 yards from our apartment, was your man with his *ANN* tattoo, reading the paper. I went into the shower and got herself to scrub as hard as she could, but to no avail – the tattoo had at least another week or two of life in it. And I spent the rest of the holiday wearing a T-shirt in the pool. Just told people I was sunburnt, but really afraid yer man would murder us. So be careful playing Spot the Irish – it can be a dangerous game.

BEWARE OF THE SALES REPS AND DEL BOYS

JS: Emma, you've never been to a foreign holiday

resort before so one thing you've got to be aware of is those people trying to lure you into the bar with free shots and low prices are not your friends. They're not doing you a favour or saving you money. They're sales reps. 'Reps' represents reptile as far as I'm aware, which will become quite apparent when they ask you 'Would you like to come in for shots?' or 'Two for one offers!' forty times a day.

'Nah, you're grand love, it's half nine in the morning, it's Irish tea I'm after.'

The best way to avoid reps is to walk the backstreets, or pretend you're a racehorse with blinkers on. If you can't see them, they're not really there.

If you hear somebody shouting 'Alright Del Boy?' from a distance, keep walking. This is of course unless you fancy buying a knock-off designer handbag or a pair of sunglasses spelt *Roy-Bon* instead of *Ray-Ban*. These men are known as Del Boys because they do more wheeling and dealing and ducking and diving than the *Only Fools and Horses* character. The key to buying from the Del Boys is to haggle. I once got quoted €50 for a watch, I'm not even good when it comes to haggling but I managed to get the watch for €3.50. Needless to say, it wasn't a Rolex.

MAKE SURE PEOPLE KNOW WHERE YOU'RE FROM

JB: My approach on a sun holiday is seven days means seven GAA jerseys. I know I'm Irish, anyone who looks at me is gonna know I'm Irish, pure pale with mad Irish hair, like I'm only down from the mountain. So I just go with it and put on my jersey. This will attract other Irish people. If they see you on the terrace of a bar in your Tipp jersey, they'll flock to the place, knowing that it can't be too bad if those Tipp lads are enjoying it. Beat that, TripAdvisor.

This is not necessarily the right approach when going to see the Sistine Chapel or the *Mona Lisa*. Equally, if you're trekking around Peru and trying not to attract attention, something less eye-catching than the Cavan training gear would be recommended. But if you choose somewhere like Spain or the Canaries in the sun, feel free to go full Irish.

We hope we've been some help to you. All that's left to do now, Emma, is to go away and enjoy yourselves.

JB: And make sure Wayne puts his hand in his pocket the odd time.

JS: That's rich coming from you.

THE GYM

Dear Johnnies,

How are the lads? Love the podcasts and hearing people writing in with all their mad problems though I wouldn't be one for writing into radio shows or that kind of thing. My brother once won a bike on The Den but other than that I'm under the radar.

My problem is straightforward. I'm outta shape. We were looking at the pictures from a family wedding five years ago and I was only a whippet. I started working full-time as a rep for a hardware supplies company. I'm on the road five days a week, fairly fond of the goujons and the fizzy pop. I wasn't long getting what we call in the business, a 'car arse'. Myself and the girlfriend broke up just after Christmas too. As ye would say, 'negative waves', but seeing that photo of how I used to be, shook me. I'm in bad shape, lads, and I don't know where to start. I'm not a fan of the gym – fair play to the lads who go but I just think there'd be too many people looking at themselves in the mirror and looking at me, and I not knowing what I'm at. Really don't like the thought of going in there, but if not there, then where do I start?

Thanks lads, keep up the good work.

Joe on the road

JS: Joe my friend, you've come to the right place. If there's anyone who knows about health and fitness, it's two Junior A hurling, joke-telling, song-singing, podcasting authors from Tipperary.

JB: Joe, we feel your pain, it's an easy happen. When we left our jobs and went full-time at *The 2 Johnnies*, we both put on weight. It wasn't fizzy pop we were drinking either. Guinness is full of iron. It's also full of calories. It took us at least a year to adjust to our new lifestyle and develop a routine that worked for us.

Having to work out of the car five days a week is tough. Back in the day the only places in which you could get food would have been pubs. Pull in for a steak dinner and a pint and drive away cos it was the eighties and Ireland was like *The Dukes of Hazzard*. In the late nineties the breakfast-roll boom exploded onto the Irish culinary scene. It was like crack cocaine to builders. There was no more bringing sandwiches to work – it was down to the petrol station for all the fried pork products you could manage. Then come lunchtime it was the chicken fillet roll – Ireland's national dish.

Only recently have your options on the road changed, Joe. If you walk into a deli, it's now perfectly acceptable for a grown man to order a salad. When we were young, the only people we saw eating a salad were them women in *Sex and the City*. We just assumed men weren't allowed eat them. We thought we'd get some sort of reaction and grow a pair of boobs if we ate lettuce.

Joe, a man in your situation (siting down so much) doesn't need all the carbohydrates you get from breakfast rolls followed by a chicken fillet roll two hours later. Try a salad sometime, you'll feel all the better for it.

Below is the best advice you could possibly buy in a comedy book for €12.99. We've got your back, we've got your shoulders, we've got your legs. Don't skip legs, Joe. We've got your abs, they're in there. We're gonna get you looking and feeling better. Trust us – as sure as Brian Cody wears a hat, when your ex-girlfriend sees you walking round with your new look, she's gonna be hungry for a hot cup of Joe.

It isn't going to be easy, but you can't run a marathon without taking the first step.

ALTERNATIVE WAYS TO START GETTING FIT

Five-a-side soccer

Somewhere close to every medium-sized town is an all-weather pitch. 'Astro' some people call it, as if we're going kicking soccer in outer space like. On that plastic pitch you'll see lads playing soccer. It's fairly casual. If these lads were actually serious about it, they'd be playing for a club. Overweight van drivers, frustrated dads, beer merchants who used to be talented, they're all going to be on show here. Ask your friends – they probably already have a game going and haven't asked you cos you haven't moved your legs in about six years. Even if you're about as much use as a cardboard cut-out of Derek Mooney at right back, just join in. Run around, break a sweat, don't break any bones. Local soccer leagues bring out some super team names too so that should keep you entertained. Some of our favourite soccer team names in Ireland are Atletico Ardfert and Ballymac Galaxy in Kerry, Bayern Mooney in Ballymoney, Co. Antrim, and Brayzil in Wicklow.

Cycle

If you're gonna do it, in the name of Joe Dolan, will you buy the padded shorts. We took part in a charity cycle from Adare to Cahir, 78 km with no training.

JS: I arrived on with more gear than U2, more Lycra than a Madonna video, sunglasses – the whole shebang.

JB: I on the other hand did it in a full Tipperary GAA tracksuit and an old Cooper hurling helmet. I also didn't realise the bike I borrowed from a neighbour had gears on it. It was only on arriving in Cahir that I realised I'd done the whole race in fifth gear.

All fun and games at the time, but the next day your arse will feel like Larry Mullen played the back catalogue on you with his new steel drumsticks. Unless you want to walk like John Wayne, get padded shorts.

Maybe borrow a bike to see if you like it and are gonna make it a regular thing. Many a fella took a notion in January and spent €1,500 on a racing bike thinking they were gonna conquer the Alps, only to find they didn't really enjoy it and ended up flogging the bike on DoneDeal for a loss. If you're gonna cycle, please do it single file and obey the rules of the road. There's a few lads down our way and I swear the Hells Angels would be easier to pass.

JS: I knocked down three or four of them and all of a sudden I'm the bad guy. Excuse me.

Walk

JB: It's like stealing your neighbour's newspaper, we all do it.

JS: Ah lad, is that where you've been getting them?

JB: Ok, my bad. Sorry to Tom and Patricia next door. But the thing to remember here is we can all walk.

A quickie at lunch? Don't mind if we do, even if it's only around the block. Then in the evening try to do a half hour. It won't have you looking like the Terminator but it's a start, and even the Terminator had to start somewhere.

Join a club

Yes, people voluntarily meet up to run around the countryside. Anyone can join these clubs. No matter how bad you think you are, Joe, you won't be finishing last. You can take pride in knowing that no matter how unfit you are, there's always some other poor bastard in even worse shape. Joining a running, badminton, tennis or any non-contact sport club is a safe and fun way to start. We've never played badminton but because we play hurling, we assume we'd be class at it.

JS: I reckon if I played it once I'd get called up for the Olympics.

Start at home

If you're lacking the confidence to go to the gym or it

feels like an intimidating place then try starting at home. Look on YouTube. This will get you going and after a while of just you and the dog, you may feel ready to work out in front of other people, i.e. in the gym or running on the road.

JB: I often work out to the videos of gym star Joe Wicks. He's so much fun that it makes the workout more enjoyable. I think Joe and I are going to be great friends. I feel like I already know him. Don't know why he's not answering my phone calls. Come on Mr Wicks, hit me up!

Now, if you've followed those guidelines, we think it's time you hit your local gym. It seems a scary place, but so did secondary school. It's just like that all over again. It was tough at the start but got easier and you went along. You'll also come across the odd tosser, just like school, but don't let that take your eyes off the prize. You'll be right at home if you adhere to the following:

Do: Bring a towel

If you're doing it right, you'll sweat like mad. Don't be dripping all over the bike like the front row of a Michael Bublé concert. Bring a small towel, the kind your aunt would rob from a hotel: keeps your face dry, stops the sweat getting into your eyes. Good gym etiquette.

Do: Be careful who you take advice from

Just cos someone looks like they know what they're doing, doesn't mean they do. It was lads in suits and €50 haircuts who messed up the banking sector, so just cos a fella has a Gym Shark vest on and massive arms doesn't mean he has a degree in his pocket.

Do: Talk to a professional

Joe, I too hate spending money, but a few sessions with a professional will be time well spent. They'll assess you, give you advice and show you how to do the exercises correctly. If you go in gung-ho, horsing dumb-bells like you're swatting flies, you'll get injured. That's the one thing you want to avoid. You'll say, 'Don't mind that gym, I only got hurt up there' and you'll never go back.

Don't be shy about asking questions – they've heard it all before and hey, that's their job.

Do: Go with a friend

I know a man who talks so much that the factory where he works actually had to put him on the night shift on his own so he couldn't distract anyone. That's not the friend you want to go to the gym with. You want someone who'll say,

'Hey, get out of bed, you bastard.' And you'll have plenty of opportunities to repay the favour as we all have those days.

Do: Wear headphones

If you're by yourself, bring your own music. The music typically played in gyms is like something robbed from a Soviet-era disco. Dodgy dance music and remixes of songs that were happy enough not to be remixed. If you can, get headphones that will cover your ears and block out the noises of whatever's going on around you. This will help you concentrate and forget about the pain!

Also, buy good runners. Johnny B climbed Galtee Moor in a pair of four-year-old Sambas and how he didn't break his neck is a miracle.

Do: Go early in the morning

I know getting up early isn't for everyone. Smacks won't do it unless it's to catch a bargain-price flight to somewhere serving cocktails with little umbrellas on them. But it *is* a super start to the day. When you've been good in the morning you're less likely to crack and order chocolate cake for lunch. It also kick-starts your metabolism so you have more energy and be less likely to gulp them sugary drinks you used to crave. Our gym is like a beehive in the evening, jointed like the jacks in the old Páirc uí Chaoimh. Go early, go hard and go home. Forty-five minutes will do you Joe. Ease into it.

And remember to enjoy it.

Don't: Take steroids

It may seem like a shortcut to being totally jacked. But when your head grows to the size of three-gallon bucket and you email the Chinese lad you bought them off, you could find the customer service below par. This may seem far-fetched, but statistically there's probably a lad in your gym on the juice, and we don't mean grapefruit (which is lovely and very good for you).

Steroids are totally unregulated. You have no idea what's in them. Could be auld bits of sawdust and rats' tails. Your journey to being healthy and fit is just that, a journey. Walk one step at a time and don't take a lift in the back of a van – you wouldn't know where you'll end up.

Don't: Just do what you like doing

Lads like to fill out the arms of a T-shirt. It's the one spot that just can't be tight enough. Tight on the arms, loose on the gut, like Eoin Kelly and Lar Corbett, a magic combination. If all you do is the stuff you like doing, like arms and chest, then you'll have big arms and chest. You'll end up like Popeye.

Arms like a JCB, lung capacity of a Starlet Boxy. Don't skip leg day, or cardio, or stretching. You want to get toned, but you also want to have your own knees when you're fifty.

Don't: Go supplement-mad

Pre-workout supplements sounds like fun. If they use words like *Crazy* and *Beast* on the packet, with an absolute lack of clarity on what's actually happening inside, then caution is to be advised. I got a free sample once, swallowed the whole thing and off I went to the gym. After twenty minutes my head felt like a bottle of 7 Up. Thought my heart was gonna burst outta my Tipp jersey and onto the floor, and if it had, I would've drop-kicked it out the window I was so pumped. This stuff gives you short-term energy and is probably fine when used correctly, but Joe, you aren't togging out to fight Conor McGregor. You don't need crazy beast mode just yet.

Don't: Try keep up with other people

Everyone is competitive, especially men in the gym. If you try overtake a Formula One car in a '91 Fiesta, you'll burn out the engine and have to drop it out to Johnny Two-Stroke to get it fixed. And he's a disaster, put bits off a sewing machine into my sister's Corolla. Still goes, but you have to change the spool of wool every fifty miles.

Ignore what other lads are doing, Joe. Push yourself a little and don't be afraid of being a little stiff or sore in a day or two, that's totally natural. Warm up, stretch, consult your trainer and never mind the begrudgers.

Don't: Be posting flat out on social media

Not many people know this, but if you go to the gym and don't put it on Instagram, it still actually works just fine. No harm if you want to track your progress, but please don't be taking your top off to take photos in the mirror. You are not Dwayne 'The Rock' Johnson, no matter how many inspirational quotes you post. Your friends and family will support you, and if they don't, just kick them in the face and give them one of the inspirational quotes you got off YouTube: 'A pheasant is just a turkey until it learns to spread its wings' or 'Keep her between the ditches', something like that.

Don't: Starve yourself

You want to lose weight, sound. You can do this by cutting down on the really bad stuff. Maybe instead of your weekend being twenty-five large bottles of cider and a doner kebab, you could try drinking less. At this point, some people will horse this book out the window. It's just a suggestion.

Don't ever be going around the place hungry. If you're exercising, you'll be hungry after that and you'll need good food to recover. Your PT will help you out. If in doubt, go for Mammy's dinner, she won't put you wrong. Also, what the fuck are you doing taking advice off two Junior B comedians?

WHO YOU'LL MEET

You're not to be scared of who you'll meet at the gym, Joe. Here's a look at who you can expect to be seeing in there:

String vest guy

There's a 75 per cent chance his name is Craig. There's a 99 per cent chance he shaves his chest.

I don't mind a trim. One of our mates has a back like the Amazon – you'd swear there's a tribe of villagers living under his shirt. You don't want that, but you probably don't need to start shaving or waxing yet. The idea behind it is that it makes your chest look more toned. If you see a nineteen-year-old lad with his top off at a festival, he'll have a chest as smooth as a snooker ball.

String vest guy is probably in good shape. He wears an impractically skimpy garment to show off his shaved and toned upper body. But what he may not know is that everyone else in the room thinks he's a donkey, with all the personality of scrambled egg. Unless you're dressing up as Hulk Hogan and may need to rip off your top and execute a leg drop at any moment, a string vest is not a good choice. Please wear something more modest to the gym.

String vest guy is to be avoided like a fart.

The mammies

They arrive around 10 a.m., after the school run is done and with all the built-up frustration of your dad trying to fix a printer. Usually in packs of twos or threes. They'll pound the treadmill, bike, or use the stairclimbing thing for an angry twenty minutes, then spend another twenty minutes giving out about the neighbours, teachers, binmen, kids, neighbour's kids, cousin's dog, husband, and any of the other mammies who aren't currently in the room. It seems they haven't the slightest idea of what they're at in the gym.

They just angrily attack the cross-trainer like it owes them money. The mammies will never enter the weights room. They don't want to get 'all big'. Cardio and sit-ups are the order of the day, every day. Work out beside the mammies for a while, it's great craic to eavesdrop on them. It's also where we source our material.

The grunter

He's big, he lifts heavy weights and he sounds like a tyrannosaurus.

JB: There's a tennis player from Argentina called Carlos Berlocq. He grunts every time he hits the ball. Like my auld lad trying to start a chainsaw. No one likes listening to Ronan Keating, chainsaws or Carlos Berlocq, so please don't grunt like a madman in the gym. Remember to breathe out on every exertion. Save the dinosaur impressions for when you become lead singer in a heavy metal band.

The phone guy

Why is he here? Who's he hiding from? In every gym there will be a guy not really sure of what he's doing, not working very hard, just there in body.

There was a lad when we went to the gym, I swear to god, we'd be a good half hour into our workout before he'd emerge from the dressing room. What was he doing? The men's changing room of a gym is not the place you want to spend your mornings. The smell of bleach and stale sweat doesn't help and the view is of big hairy arses in the shower. It's a quiet place. No one talks to each other unless they are close friends. I don't know if you've ever tried to strike up a chat with a naked middle-aged man, but eye contact is key.

There are people who sit on the one machine, on their phone, stealing oxygen and paying 70 quid a month for the privilege. Don't be one of those people. 'I go to the gym' – ya, my ma goes to mass but that doesn't make her the Pope.

Get in, work out, then enjoy your day. You can stare at your phone for free at home.

The Eastern European meat men

In our town there's a meat factory. Most of the lads who work there are from Eastern Europe.

JB: We call them Polish, they're probably not and are offended by that but they're not the target market of this book so it'll be grand.

JS: Looks like there won't be a live show in Gdansk next year.

They land into the gym around half four and start pumping iron. They do not run. They do not cycle; they do not use that stairs thing. They lift heavy weights. I think it's fair to say most of the Polish lads have more confidence than us Irish boys – it's just the way we are from Mammy and the Church giving out to us all our lives. But these lads are body-confident. Happy to check themselves out in the mirror, discuss their progress with their gym buddies, strike a few poses and point to a newly formed line in their triceps. If an Irishman did that, you'd revoke his citizenship. I get on fine with these lads. They're happy to share any weights or machines. They do talk awfully loud though. In Poland until 2009 every young male had to do nine months of military service. I wonder were there a lot of explosives going off and they're now hard of hearing? I can't tell what they're saying, they sound like the bad guys from *Taken*. Probably just having the craic but I can see how you might find this intimidating. Stick to your plan, work hard, the time will fly.

The GAA lads

They mostly don't know what they're doing and aren't going to ask either. If you see a skinny lad doing sit-ups, or a heavy lad lifting big weights but only three or four reps, they may be a junior GAA player after hearing about the wonders of the gym. We soldiered for years in our club with a guy nicknamed 'The Octopus' cos he was so gangly. He had the posture of a sick calf. He walked into the gym like he'd been carried there inside a suitcase and was now unable to straighten up. A gym instructor's nightmare. In a group of twenty, the instructor gave 90 per cent of his time trying to show The Octopus the correct way to perform a squat. The instructor reconsidered his life choices after that session and The Octopus never came back. He can't squat, but you won't catch a ball over him.

The GAA lads are fit, but often lacking flexibility and core strength so when they go to the gym, they just do arms and chest. Exercises they saw on Instagram or something one of the Polish lads was doing and he looked good so it was worth a go. The GAA lads are usually just like yourself, Joe, not really at home in the gym, happier on the pitch, pucking ball or kicking wides, but the Dublin footballers are all in the gym, so now your local Junior A cornerback is in the gym too.

The leggings chicks

Joe, there will be ladies in the gym, beautiful ladies – not all the time, this isn't Coppers – and sometimes these ladies will be wearing leggings so tight Houdini wouldn't get out of them. A woman wouldn't wear them to mass – she'd turn the priest – but in the gym, they're spot on. The gym is fashionable now and most young women are in good shape. Instagram has them all driven mad. They could be called to participate in *Love Island* at any minute. You may feel nervous sweating your ass off beside the leggings ladies, but you'll get over it, Joe. They'll be self-conscious too and it's not a bad place to get talking to a girl either. Yer both out of yer comfort zone and have at least one thing in common. But if a girl is squatting nearby and she catches you staring at her arse, you'll have to leave the country and never return. Cool? Knock 'em dead.

Joe, we hope this has helped. Now be bold, get up off that couch, put down this book (pick it back up later, it gets better) and take that first step to a happier, healthier you.

JB: As my father used to say, 'A change is as good as a vest.'

JS: I'm sure we'll see you on next year's *Love Island* or *Crimewatch*. It could go either way.

HAVING A BABY

Dear Johnnies,

Hiya lads, serious enough question here: my missus has been putting a lot of pressure on me lately about us having kids. We're together three years and it's great like, but I have to admit I'm not really sure I'm ready for the whole kids thing yet.

I play music for a living. It's good auld craic – weddings, pubs, you name it, I've sung there. I have an original project on the go too, not sure if it's going anywhere but it's there nonetheless and I love playing. I'm a drummer as well so not exactly ideal conditions for raising a baby in the house. It's currently filled with my instruments, heavy-metal CDs and vinyl collections. I don't want to lose herself over this. I think I'll get there in time. I just don't know when that time is. I feel like maybe I don't have my life in order so how could I look after another little life? It could be grand like, sure how do you ever know if you're ready?

Some advice on how to figure this out, while keeping things cool with the missus, would be much appreciated, boys.

Peace out,

Barry, Limerick

Barry, my man, you seem like a good guy, and being 'almost musicians' ourselves, we can relate. You need to assess your life and your relationship, and see if you're ready to take this gig to the next level. In the meantime, we suggest getting her a dog. A right prick of a dog. The kind that sustains itself solely by digesting the lining of your couch. The kind that barks at the sad parts of the movie and that does its business on her kitchen floor. That'll soften her cough. A few weeks of living with an underachieving dog and she may hold off on having a baby for a while. A baby is a big commitment, you can't send it back to the shop so. Here are some more areas of your life that may need consideration:

Sessions

Would you be fond of a pint? Not to make assumptions here, but most musicians we know are pure Jerry Hound Dogs on the beer. I think it's the frustration of playing a wedding sober, watching everyone else having a good time and you're pounding the drums all night. If it was a country and western band you were in, I'd say you'd be reaching for the spirits as soon as you got off stage! A fine musician like yourself playing Daniel O'Donnell all night – trust us, you'd be gone brain dead.

When you do get a chance to go out? Do you go hard? Are you welded to the couch the following day? Cos newsflash,

Barry, a newborn don't give a damn about your hangover. When you're drooling all over the settee, the baby isn't going to wipe you clean and order a 3 in 1 from the Chinese. You can put the dog outside or tell him not to eat the remote but a baby human requires genuine attention. When they cry, they aren't doing it for the craic. They may have shat themselves, and you'll to clean it up. Are you prepared to do it while hungover?

JB: I ate a banana in front of my hungover friend one day. Had to pull over the van cos he was gagging. He couldn't handle fruit, never mind poo. So you'll find yourself going out less because the hangover just isn't worth it. And when you do go out, you'll be drinking less in an attempt to be some way able to tackle the little person the next day.

JS: I've seen grown men reduced to tears on the way home from a stag weekend knowing they had to face into a three-hour *Peppa Pig* marathon on arrival.

Find a good babysitter and don't go full Shane McGowan on your nights out. You should be ok.

Work

Your job is a tricky one, you'll be getting in late at night. You'll have to creep around the house trying not to wake the baby. The next morning when you need to sleep in, surprise – there's a child in your face and it feels like being loud. If you find changing the skins on your drum kit a hard slog, then get ready for changing nappies. Also, no one's trying to take a leak on you while changing the drum skins. Though that depends on where the gig is, I suppose.

Would you be open to the idea of changing your career? Taking gigs that finish earlier, like school musicals and other soul-destroying events? How about teaching? You can bestow your love of Slayer onto the next generation of students.

Money

A pair of Adidas Predator Precision football boots costs about €250. Amount of times a child defecates on itself in a year? About 1,800 times. In turn, the price of 1,800 nappies, about €250.

A set of Sabian HH cymbals for your drum kit works out at €979. A week's supply of Happy Baby organic baby food, €20. That's over a grand a year.

Tickets to see Bob Dylan, €104. Hotel for the night, €95. Flake of pints, let's say €80 (includes chips). Hangover food, €20. Total €299. Every baby needs a pram, €300.

Then there are other costs. They seem to grow fairly fast, so you'd be as well off getting all second-hand clothes. Hit up your family, your neighbours, the charity shops. Baby isn't gonna argue, 'Aw Daddy, I don't wear Penneys runners, they must be Nikes.'

Babies sleep in a little bed with bars around the sides. Mountjoy job – they call it a cot. Dog can't get in, child can't get out. That's a hundred quid anyway.

And remember the child won't know what a toy is – just give them things lying round the house to play with. As long as they're not kitchen knives or live cables, you'll be grand.

JS: I always found a set of keys to be amusing, and I turned out fine.

JB: That's debatable.

Anyone you see wearing a pair of €180 runners is not a parent or else they're a famous rapper and a part-time parent. Kanye West has kids and fancy runners, but he sold 21 million albums, he's not playing the lounge of Hotel Kilkenny every second Friday. It's going to be a period of adjustment, Barry. One of these days you'll hear the pitter-patter of tiny drains on your resources.

Hobbies and sport

We see lads trying to be involved in GAA when they have kids and it's not easy. It's always the same. Jimmy can't be a selector; the wife just had a baby. Few months of that and you can be sure Jimmy will be volunteering to be manager of any team going. Junior B, under-12 camogie, carrying water for the fellas lining the field, you name it, Jimmy will do it. A bit of fresh air never did a man any harm.

We had a manager who used to bring his son to all the games. Young fella was only three or four, he was no use as a selector but it saved our manager having to pay a babysitter. There was one match and we weren't playing well at all. At half-time the manager called us all into a big circle on the field. He was roaring at us, really tearing strips out of guys and questioning their commitment to the club and their hunger as athletes. It was all serious stuff. Then we noticed his kid had wandered into the middle of the circle, sucking on a lollipop, pants down, lad out, taking a nice pee for himself on the grass, not a care in the world. Needless to say, that team talk didn't have the desired effect!

I once saw a man referee the final of the local parish league – he had the referee's whistle in his mouth and a child under each arm – and they say men can't multitask. He was under some pressure. The strangest thing was, his wife was on the sideline on her own.

Your all-night computer-game marathons are on thin ice now too, Barry, because you'll soon put a premium on sleep. *Metal Gear Solid* can't compete with Sleeping Solid for Seven Hours.

Whatever about bringing a kid to football practice, you can't bring it to band practice. It's not the 110 decibels of rock 'n' roll, it's the crusty wretches playing it. If you leave your child alone with a few musicians, there's a good chance you'll come back to see it with a cigarette in its mouth and a microphone taped to its head. They'll be after turning it into a sample to use on a new song or something. 'Great resonance off that baby, maaan.'

Which is why you need to consider:

Have you someone you can dump the child on?

This is where your parents come in handy. You've probably thought, 'Ah I'll never live beside them.' Introduce a baby into the equation and you may find them very useful all of a sudden. Childcare is expensive. If you live close enough to your parents, you can call in for a nice social call and be like, 'Hey I must just pop into town there for a minute and buy some new, ah, lawnmowers, will you mind the baby?' They've got the qualifications. Look how well you turned out.

Is it a deal-breaker?

If you say to your good lady that you're not ready for a few years, is she gonna do a Meatloaf and be gone like a bat out of hell? Hopefully the dog with the learning disability will slow her roll for a while, giving you time to think.

And here's hoping that she loves you enough to wait for you, and help you along that road. If you have children just because someone has pressured you into it, it'll end badly. The peer pressure that made you smoke your first fag at fifteen was bad, but you can give up the cigarettes. This child is for life. It shouldn't be brought into the world until it has a loving environment in which to grow up. We got a bit serious there, Barry. Tell her chill out, you sort your shit out and it'll be grand.

POSITIVES TO HAVING A BABY

Picking names

You get to name the child! Remember how much fun you had naming your band? This is even better. Give your child a strong name that they can really own. If you name the boy Paddy, he's going to be a coalman, or a tour guide on a Paddy Wagon, showing old Americans around Killarney. If you name her Scarlet she'll be trouble, stuck in her room singing songs about how she wants to stab you, and she'll definitely be smoking fags out the back of school. We recommend you play it safe. Call him Gary and let him be a mechanic.

Teaching them crazy stuff

Guaranteed your mother told you carrots helped you see in the dark so that you would eat them. Bugs Bunny ate them orange yokes all day and what was inside his rabbit hole? A big lamp. Bullshit.

JB: I'm going to tell my kids that ginger people are actually made of chocolate and if they run up and bite them hard enough, they'll taste it. Should be gas craic.

JS: I'll tell them monkeys used to look like us but then they moved to Carlow. After years of having to survive in Carlow IT they grew strong and hairy. It was the only way to manage in Scraggs Alley.

IS YOUR HOUSE BABY READY?

Housemates

Do you live with your mates? They all have to go.

JB: As one of my former house mates said, 'Dogs, maybe. Cats, no. Kids, fuck no.'

Your typical baby is useless to drink. Contributes absolutely nothing to a session. A craic vacuum. You may as well not invite them. What happens when the baby drops a log and you have to change its shitty nappy? You can't do it in the sitting room, wiping up scutter and the boys trying to watch the Champions League final. The smell would blow the head off them.

If your typical Sunday night involves coming home from the pub drunk, singing 'Come Out ye Black and Tans', pouring peanut butter on your chips and walking round the house with a hurley in your hand in case the ghost of

Margaret Thatcher shows up, that's perfectly fine when it's just a bunch of friends in the gaff. If there's a baby in the shake-up then that ain't gonna fly.

JS: I suppose you could make a lullaby version of a few rebel songs, but if your three-year-old rocks into playschool singing 'The Men Behind the Wire', they're gonna get some looks.

Noise

We don't mean to sound like Team America vs the Taliban, but kids hate everything you love. Rock 'n' roll is toxic to them. They'll do everything in their power to destroy it. That 1975 handmade Gibson 'Les Paul' guitar you have hanging on the wall, with the sunburst mahogany body and custom pick-ups – if a kid gets their hands on that, it's coming down. Right on top of them. And not in some kind of cool way like Nirvana smashing a guitar on stage at Glastonbury. Expensive musical memorabilia has to be put well out of reach, Barry.

A bad kid is more rebellious than The Sex Pistols and Mötley Crüe any day. 'Eat your breakfast.' 'No.' 'Why not like, what are you, too busy shitting yourself?'

JB: I knew a lad who took up the bagpipes. He couldn't practise in the house cos it was incredibly loud. He had to find a compromise so he marched up and down the street in full costume and told people it was part of his religion.

JS: Drumming while the baby is in the house is probably out of the question. I recommend you buy the child a pair of those noise-cancelling earmuffs. They'd act as a ball and chain to stop them from wandering off cos with the weight of them, the child won't be able to lift its head.

Escape

By the time the child is a year old, it'll probably be walking and trying to go full Tom Crean Antarctic explorer every morning. It's your job to stop them. You have to lock the external doors and windows. Yes, locks on every window like it's a Brazilian hostel. The baby might try jump out the window, just for the craic. If they fall then you'll get some daggers off the ambulance crowd. It's just not worth it, lad.

You have to put some sort of device on the garden gates too, if you have them. The gate at the end of the stairs is another potential war zone. By the age of two, they'll be able to climb up on it, so it's better not swing open with them on it or child services will be at the front door. They can go on an absolute rampage and whatever damage they do is your fault.

It's like bringing your crazy cousin to your mate's stag. They do the crime, you pay the fine.

Appliances

JB: When I was three, I climbed up on the TV and ended up dragging it down on top of myself. It wasn't the *Star Trek*-looking flat screens you have nowadays, but a big rear-projection block of a machine that probably saw the moon landing. My poor mother thought I was dead. I laughed it off and the TV also survived for another fifteen years but it could have been the end of me. Took years before I got back on TV again.

Sharp knives have to be locked away. Even the toilet may have to have one of them child-lock yokes on it. Some kids will drink out of the toilet, I swear to god. You'd give out to the dog if he did it.

Leaving your laptop on the table while still plugged in is not an option. The baby's gonna pull it down. Your phone left on a chair? There's a 60 per cent chance it ends up in the jacks. You'll start to wonder why anything has sharp edges. You know that saying about playing with fire? A baby came up with that, immediately forgot it and burned themselves again.

Those cables on your window blinds, you'll have to tie a knot in them. You'll probably start to think it's not the only thing you should be tying a knot in, Barry.

JS: If it were me, I would consider moving into a bouncy castle for the first couple of years.

Living with the missus

Sex on tap. Try it now: walk over to the sink, turn on the tap, what comes out? That's right. Hot sex. Young couples living together, ye're still getting it on. Now, between tears and naps, adult time will have to be planned to precision. What if she breastfeeds? Ask yourself, Barry, are you ready to share the tit? Are you also ready to share the bed? We know babies are small, but put one in your bed and it'll swell like industrial expanding foam. You'd be surprised how much room a kid can take up.

Pets

JB: My dog, Bob Marley, is about as much of a child as I can handle. He likes to play with his sliotar, eat timber and chase birds. We get on just fine. When he wants to go for a pee, he stands up at the door and gives me a look. It's in both our interests to let him out. If your dog isn't well trained and is gonna bark every five minutes, then you have an issue. My granny said there were healing powers in a dog's lick, but you can't let the dog lick the child, the mother will go mad. Actually, that could have been a dock leaf.

JS: As for anything mad like a pet snake or a parrot, let the snake out down the town, he'll be grand, town is full of snakes anyway. Any form of birds (parrots, budgies, etc.) should be popped in the oven for Sunday roast and peace and quiet.

Now it's time to get all Jerry Springer on you, Barry. At the end of the day, a child is a wonderful thing to bring into the world. But you better be ready to raise it right.

JB: An auld boy I worked with used to tell me before I went out on a job, 'Wherever you go, don't bring an eejit with you, cos there'll already be one there.'

JS: Barry, the world is already full of mad bastards

going around getting into trouble, eating crayons down the back of class. We have enough of them, if you're going to give us another human, give us a good one. Until then, wrap it up!

Dear Johnnies,

Sinead here from Mullingar. My problem is not my own. It's about my sister. She's 18, a few years younger than me and while I've been away in college and travelling, I've returned home to realise she's become some sort of wannabe blogger. We've always been a bit different. I prefer a can of cider, she's drinking gin out of a fishbowl down the local. She's a really girlie girl, which is fine, but lately she's been posting every day on her Instagram like she's Kylie Jenner and talking about make-up and hair products and I'm like, 'What does she know about it?'

I suppose lots of 18-year-olds these days are mad into make-up, sticking on eyelashes, fake tan, taking 50 selfies so she can get the right one. It's harmless fun, to a point, but she takes it to heart if a photo doesn't get enough likes. She spends forever on her phone, editing photos so she looks better and I just feel this can't be healthy.

How can I get her head out of her phone and get her back happy and living in the real world?

Sinead

Mullingar

Hi Sinead,

Thanks for getting in touch. Without yer problems we'd have no book.

We would say not to worry too much yet – your sister is young and still finding her way in the world. She sounds like she's absolutely no craic to be honest, but fair play to you for trying to look after her. Too much of that social media will have you gone mad. We know a young lad doing his apprenticeship, he's the only carpenter we've seen taking a break while cutting a 2x1. He can't go two minutes without checking the phone. No good. It's a habit young people have at the moment, checking their phone while you're trying to talk to them. It's the height of ignorance and if our kids did it to us, the phone or the child would be out the window. Thankfully, we don't have any kids yet.

We've got some aspects of your problem we'd like to dissect, just click on the link to see the article. Oh, wait – this isn't social media.

WHY BECOME A BLOGGER/INFLUENCER?

It sounds like your sister doesn't have an interest outside of general blogging, and no specific subject she's an expert on and can blog about. The world of female influencers is a place in which we feel very uncomfortable. For us guys to talk about it is like doing a reading when making your confirmation: if we say the wrong thing, we won't get away with it. But our publishers said we needed another chapter, so here goes.

We don't really understand why women do it. We can take the argument that 'it's great fun' to a point. I don't know just how much fun it is to take forty selfies, then put the best on Instagram and check your phone every minute to see how many likes it has. Your sister needs a hobby. She wouldn't be on her phone if she was out playing the banjo or lamping rabbits. Get a bit of fresh air into her.

Then there's the 'I get loads of free stuff' reason.

JB: Getting free stuff is great. I often get free goujons at the local deli by tipping them into the bag with my jambon and just using the one sticker. #livingmybestlife

JS: That's just illegal.

INSTAGRAM VS REALITY

Instagram: Hi guys, so a lot of people have been asking about my moisturising routine, and I just thought I'd take a moment to show all my followers what my secret is.

Reality: No one was asking about your routine! The finale of *Riverdance*, now that was a routine. You're just cleaning your face, which is a good thing, but you don't have to hold a press conference from your bedroom. If you come across something that people may find helpful and you'd like to share it with them, then work away, but don't pretend that you're like Bruce Springsteen, back by popular demand.

Instagram: Photo of a pizza box, captioned *Love these lazy Sundays.*

Reality: You haven't eaten a carbohydrate since Junior Cert. This one drives us crazy, Instagrammers pretending to eat junk food when they don't. There's people at home watching that thinking, 'How does that bitch eat pizza and still stay skinny?' They don't. Instagram is the highlight reel. What people put on the internet is not an accurate picture.

Instagram: Photo of hot young wan in the gym, captioned *Excuse the tomato head on me #gains.*

Reality: She doesn't have a tomato head on her because she hasn't done a tap yet. Any woman who's been to the gym will know the feeling of being roasting hot, covered in sweat and a face like a Cork GAA jersey. It's good to encourage others to stay active, but be honest, ye can't all have big arses like them famous wans in America. I heard some of them arses are fake anyway.

Instagram: Having such a great night with my #besties here @ [tags some place trying to get in free next time]. The next seven stories are her friends looking cat and her looking fab.

Reality: If you were having such a good time, you wouldn't be posting forty photos of your night out, while you were still on your night out. We don't stop in the middle of a hurling match and ask the ref to take a selfie with us cos our jersey looks cute. We go out and hurl the match and if the club pro puts a photo of you in action onto the club's Facebook page, then great, you can use it for Tinder. If not, hurl away. Enjoy your night, not the photos of your night.

SIGNS YOU'RE ADDICTED TO SOCIAL MEDIA

You bring it to bed

Many of us do it, but the only thing you should be bringing to bed is a cup of tay, a good book and your other half.

If you're using your smartphone, which most phones now are (if you're using an old brick Nokia, then like, what are you doing on it?), the blue light emitted from your screen restrains the production of melatonin, the hormone that controls your sleep/wake cycle or circadian rhythm. Reducing melatonin makes it harder to fall and stay asleep. Think about it. I want to relax and fall asleep, so I'll put a light six inches from my face and stare into it for an hour. No wonder you're dreaming about Kim Kardashian fighting a dragon. Improve your sleep. Put down the phone.

You take photos of your food

I just typed 'cup of coffee' into Google and it returned 907 billion photos of cups of coffee on the internet. I think they have it covered, no need for you to post yours. The only time we feel it's acceptable to post your food on social media is if you're at one of them Japanese places that cook it in front of you and do all the flips and tricks. Those lads are amazing. We went to one in Lanzarote and the chef was firing pieces of scrambled egg across the room at us. Hit me in the side of the head three times. He said 'Why you not catch?' I said, 'Hey, I can't score if the ball in is bad.' He's a talented man all the same, flames up to the ceiling, juggling knives. You wouldn't see it in Spar. So, unless it's something really unusual or entertaining, think before you post you food online, and just enjoy your meal.

You spend an hour in the loo

Do you have a condition? Are you blocked up like a chipper's drainpipe? If not, then why are you spending so long on the jacks? Are you on the phone to António Guterres, Secretary-General of the United Nations, trying to sort out a bit of world peace? Do you return from the lavatory and say 'Just sorted out the Syrian conflict there, all good'? Cos if you don't, then you have to ask, why spend so much time in a room with your own shit? There are eight rooms in my house, only two of them contain devices that process human waste. Some of the others, the sitting room for instance, are quite nice. Many people sit down to do their business, take out their phone – how unhygienic, I might add – and scroll aimlessly on social media until forty-five minutes later, they awaken to find red marks on their thighs and their pants down. It's like a visit to your in-laws: get in, get the job done, get out.

You do it in the company of friends

In the car. If I'm giving a lad a lift, the least he can do is tell me a few auld yarns. Make the journey go quicker. If the passenger is going to spend the journey looking down into their phone, then they can make like Fleetwood Mac and go their own way.

At the table. Friends drinking tea and chatting, the craic is flowing. One sure way to assassinate the craic is to look away from the conversation and into your phone. You're probably looking at photos of other people pretending to have the craic, when your own craic is going to waste right in front of you. Get your head out of your arse and into your craic.

In the pub. This is the cardinal sin of social media usage. If we ever own a pub, we're going to line the walls with lead so there's no phone coverage in there (be the ideal place for a stag). Phone activity on a night out should be limited to ringing an ambulance because your mate has had too many battered sausages, getting a taxi home, taking down your future wife's phone number or getting a video of a lad who's so drunk he can't talk. Other than that, there's absolutely no need to be flicking through your social channels. If you are, then either you or your company should leave.

DOS AND DON'TS OF SOCIAL MEDIA

Do: Think before you post

Did you ever stub your toe and shout 'faaaaaaaak' with the pain? Well seeing something you don't like on the internet and posting about it is like that. Except with the internet, you have time to take a deep breath before roaring, and there's no toe to mind. If you post in the heat of the moment, you may regret it.

Do: Ask permission

I once took a Snapchat of my mate on a night out. I only sent it to the few lads who were with us, but he being ten pints in thought I was making some sort of Martin Scorsese documentary about his trip to the jacks. He freaked out, roaring round the pub, 'Are you filming me?' We went for pizza and it was grand, but do ask your friends' and family's permission before posting footage of them.

Do: Consider the effects

What does this post say about you? Who's seeing it? A potential employer? Your football manager? The guards? The Russians? They watch a lot of stuff, must have some time on their hands. Be sure you can stand over anything you post, because it could be brought up when you least expect it (probably not by the Russians, but you never know).

Do: Be honest/be yourself

Most people, the Irish especially, can tell a fake. Like gone-off milk, they can smell your bullshit down the phone, and they'll instantly hate you for it, in that 'I don't know why but I hate him' kind of a way. Think of someone famous who wrecks your head. Do you really know why you hate them? It's probably because they're fake.

Do: Be realistic of your expectations

Don't expect to be Kim Kardashian overnight, selling millions of units of her new eyeliner because she tweeted about it. She has a team of people working on her image. She also had a sex tape, and your sister doesn't want that – well, your family definitely don't want your sister to have that.

Don't: Engage with trolls

Auld Timmy Dempsey (God be good to him) used to say to us, 'Wherever you go, don't bring an eejit with you, cos there'll already be one there.' There are fools everywhere and they have found their home on the internet, where they can act without consequence, insulting and trolling other users as they like. I think it was Taylor Swift who said 'haters gonna hate', her or Mike Denver, or maybe 2Pac. I can't remember, but the point is, people like to give out. If they give out about you, there's not much you can do about it, just go about your life the best you can.

Don't: Try replicate famous people

You don't live in Hollywood, You're friends with Tom Carroll the plumber, not Tom Cruise the actor. Don't try to be someone else. What works for them won't work for you.

Don't: Post nudes

Young people reading this: please don't post naked photos of yourself on the internet. This is serious. This is actually happening more than older readers would think. There is no fear of *The 2 Johnnies* posting nude photos online. We can think of more fun ways to ruin our career. But young wans can feel like everyone else is doing it so maybe they should too. Don't do it, gals. Ye're better than that. Now, if you're an adult and someone wants to pay you a fortune to do it, well then, those chicken fillet rolls won't pay for themselves.

Don't: Do things just for the 'gram

Live your life for you. Please don't go places just to get a photo, or for 'content'. Your real life is more important that your online persona. Unless you're Piers Morgan. Sometimes we reckon he only exists online and that the real Piers Morgan actually died years ago. The one we get online is just an experiment by Mark Zuckerberg.

Don't: Post when drunk

We learned this the hard way. On a St Patrick's Day trip to Scotland, we'd finished a run of gigs and we were up early for pints, having been up late for pints. We may have done a little bit of Snapchatting from the bar of The Three Sisters in Edinburgh. We may have had Guinness coming out our ears, and why did we have a hockey stick up on top of a hot-dog stand, while singing Kajagoogoo's 'Too Shy'? Who knows, but we got plenty of texts from friends telling us to take it down before we made a complete show of ourselves. It's a catchy song all the same.

Sinead, your sister is in a stage in her life where she's fairly impressionable. The world for her is dominated by social media. It makes no sense, but to your sister, this is a big deal. Her Instagram is how she expresses herself to the world. She sounds to us like a bit of a dose, to be honest, but don't give up on her. Try to explain the dangers. She has no idea who's looking at what she posts, or what they're doing with it: she could end up on a fake Tinder profile or on an ad for a Chinese beer. Loss of privacy is a big consideration, too. Having everyone know your business is weird. We have social media profiles and it's in our interest to have them for our job. But we still have guidelines. We don't post certain things. We try to protect our family and friends from internet trolls. Also, if you keep telling everyone where you are all the time, someone might rob your gaff!

Many people make a great career from social media. It is a very powerful tool and can be used for many wonderful things. She is young and we just want her to mind herself.

Consider what your employer, partner and family think, because it affects them too. Ask yourself this: if a strange guy walked up to you in work and said, 'I like that tattoo you have on your arse cheek,' would you find it weird? Well, you posted it online, don't blame him for seeing it.

Although, who says something like that? He may be mental. Mind yourself.

QUIZ ANSWERS

How Culchie Are You?
(page 114)

1. Marty Mone

2. Davy Carton

3. Clare

4. Longford

5. Galway

6. Cow

7. Green

8. Irish Countrywomen Association

9. September

10. Shanballyard and Poulmucka, which is just outside the 2 Johnnies HQ in Cahir.

11. Helen Carroll

12. Dinny Byrne

13. One o'clock

14. Clare

15. Donegal

16. 'Stalwarts of the land' (not 'Tinder for farmers')

17. Cheese

18. Midges

19. D'Unbelievables

20. A boat — not in fact a strawberry, as we thought.

ACKNOWLEDGEMENTS

A chairde go leir. Tá an áthas orm an leabhar seo a chur i láthair mhuintir na hÉireann. We haven't won an All-Ireland, but we do want to thank a few people:

To our family and our nearest and dearest for making us the men we are today (not great, but getting better like).

To our podcast producer Maura Fay, who's a friend and a mother to us. Thanks for putting up with us and keeping us on the straight and narrow.

Also to (former Miss Clare) Lauren Guilfoyle who's also played her part in the podcast and drunk copious amounts of tea along the way.

Thanks to the staff of the Boar's Head, Ryan's of Camden Street and PJ's bar in Lanzarote, where this book was crafted.

To our good friend Paul Collins for all his advice, for being the cause of several heavy nights and lastly for giving us our first paid gig.

To all our friends who have starred in our videos and cleaned up on Tinder as a result, we thank you. Ye give us the material we need to do this.

Thanks to Val in Mr Mister for making us stylish and Steve's barbers in Cahir for keeping our fades looking fresh.

To Hughie and Margaret in the Shamrock Lounge and the deli staff of Junction 14 and O'Donnell's of Cahir for keeping our bellies full. Goujons – throw 'em out, kid.

To the team who came on tour with us: Big James, Claire, Cecil (does nuttn but some man to tell a story), Jack, Edgy, Smokie, the other lad whose name we can't remember (possibly Dave), Ali, Annie, Clionagh and Brendan aka 'The King'.

Special thank you to Mr Noel Furlong. When we approached him to make an appearance on our podcast, it was only supposed to be a once-off, but the people loved Noel and he has started to love ye back, a bit. He still hates most people, especially the Russian government, which he's never explained to us. What's the story, Noel?

To Lar Corbett for scoring three goals against Kilkenny in the 2010 All-Ireland final.

To our band who gig with us, Barry 'Tropical' Wilson, Rory McCarthy, Pat Lucy and Brian Dunlea, if ye were any more laid back, ye'd be upside down.

To our management team at CWB. Ye're as crazy as we are.

To Gill Books, for giving us a book deal and trusting in us to not fuck it up. Sound.

Thanks to John Leahy, Joe Hayes and Pat Fox. No reason. Ye're just legends.

To the radio stations, TV shows, presenters and researchers who answered our calls and emails when so many others wouldn't, we appreciate ye giving us a chance, we hope no one got fired for playing us on air.

And lastly, a massive thanks to anyone who has bought this book, listened to our podcast, downloaded our songs and laughed at our sketches. This is only the start. There's plenty more craic to be had. See ye all in Coppers.